ACADEMIC LIBRARIES

Recent Titles in
New Directions in Information Management

The Alienated Librarian
Marcia J. Nauratil

The Role of the Academic Reference Librarian
Jo Bell Whitlatch

Public Administration and Decision-Aiding Software: Improving Procedure and Substance
Stuart S. Nagel, editor

Full Text Databases
Carol Tenopir and Jung Soon Ro

Automating Literacy: A Challenge for Libraries
Linda Main and Char Whitaker

Cataloging: The Professional Development Cycle
Sheila S. Intner and Janet Swan Hill, editors

Information and Information Systems
Michael Buckland

Vocabulary Control and Search Strategies in Online Searching
Alice Yanosko Chamis

Planning in the University Library
Stanton F. Biddle

The Information World of Retired Women
Elfreda A. Chatman

Insider's Guide to Library Automation: Essays of Practical Experience
John W. Head and Gerard B. McCabe, editors

Hypertext and the Technology of Conversation: Orderly Situational Choice
Susan H. Gray

ACADEMIC LIBRARIES

The Dimensions of Their Effectiveness

JOSEPH A. McDONALD
and
LYNDA BASNEY MICIKAS

New Directions in Information Management, Number 32
MICHAEL BUCKLAND, *Series Editor*

Greenwood Press
Westport, Connecticut • London

Library of Congress Cataloging-in-Publication Data

McDonald, Joseph A. (Joseph Andrew)
Academic libraries : the dimensions of their effectiveness /
Joseph A. McDonald and Lynda Basney Micikas.
p. cm.—(New directions in information management, ISSN 0887–3844 ; no. 32)
Includes bibliographical references and index.
ISBN 0–313–27269–7 (alk. paper)
1. Academic libraries—United States—Evaluation. I. Micikas, Lynda Basney. II. Title. III. Series.
Z675.U5M38 1994
027.7—dc20 93–14464

British Library Cataloguing in Publication Data is available.

Library of Congress Catalog Card Number: 93–14464
ISBN: 0–313–27269–7
ISSN: 0887–3844

First published in 1994

Greenwood Press, 88 Post Road West, Westport, CT 06881
An imprint of Greenwood Publishing Group, Inc.

Printed in the United States of America

The paper used in this book complies with the Permanent Paper Standard issued by the National Information Standards Organization (Z39.48–1984).

10 9 8 7 6 5 4 3 2 1

Copyright Acknowledgments

The authors and the publisher are grateful to the following for granting the use of material:

Information in Tables 5–1 and 5–2 reprinted from *Special Libraries*, v. 70, no. 4 (April 1979), pp. 173–178. © by Special Libraries Association.

Extracts from *Organizational Effectiveness: A Comparison of Multiple Models*, edited by Kim S. Cameron and David A. Whetten. 1983. Orlando: Academic Press.

Extracts from Cameron, Kim S. *Organizational Effectiveness: Its Measurement and Prediction in Higher Education*, Yale University, Ph.D., 1978, University Microfilms International Facsimile Edition, 1985.

For AnnMarie and Jonathan David

CONTENTS

ILLUSTRATIONS

TABLES

FIGURES

PREFACE

The genesis of the partnership which wrote this book lies in the Council on Library Resources. It was they who gave us two cooperative research grants designed to bring a teacher and a librarian together to conduct research of common interest and, not incidentally, perhaps, to teach the librarian how to do it. Crazy glue though it is, the bond still holds. The reader may well wonder what a geneticist and developmental biologist and a college and computer bureaucrat have in common. We have often wondered, ourselves, and we still may not have the answer. But we do know this. The backbone of higher education in the United States is the four year, largely undergraduate, liberal arts college. It is our conviction that here, in these institutions, the love of learning and the practice of the life of the mind are best developed and made part of our culture.

But learning and a certain kind of resilient and practical scholarship, which we believe are fundamental to what is known as an educated person, are not held in high esteem these days. A college education has become, largely, training and the accumulation of credits. Coherence in curricula is sought, but little obtained; systematic integration of learning from a consistent world-life view is even less understood and practiced.

We would like to think we are not naive, and recognize that college and university curricula will mirror life. We state nothing new in observing that intellectual life at the close of the twentieth century is the product of the intellectual and spiritual disintegration of this century and that its roots lie well into the nineteenth century.

One of the acts of alienation on campus has been the increasing disassociation of learning from the information environment in which it is, inevitably, embedded. Both the teacher and the information professional (librarian and media and computer specialists) are to blame, but it probably started with the rise of modern librarianship and the increasing separation between a learning perspective and an "information" perspective.

It is our desire that this book contribute to a better understanding of the relationship between learning and the information environment. And, specifically, we hope that librarians and members of various faculties can gain new insight into the integrality of learning and information, of the classroom and the library.

We extend our thanks to all those who helped make this book possible. We thank our patient families and colleagues in Philadelphia, Denver, and Malibu. We especially thank Michael Buckland for his interminable arguments that forced us to be better and better and John Minter, of John Minter Associates, who reviewed and gave valuable advice on the psychometric tests used on our data. Finally, but hardly least, a most heartfelt thank you to John Van Dyk, philosopher, teacher, world traveller, a friend who sticks closer than a brother.

Chapter 1

INTRODUCTION

"Effectiveness" can easily be defined in general terms, as accomplishing tasks in ways that promote the well-being of an organization, its members, and its constituencies. However, librarians have not been able to agree on a meaning for "library effectiveness" that is both comprehensive and practical, expressed in terms that suggest directions for improvement. Although much is said about evaluation and performance measures, the discussion generally leaves key terms undefined or leaves the reader to infer that the writers have effectiveness in mind. For example, Rogers (1954) refers to "competent and courteous service" as an effectiveness measure, and Carnovsky (1955) refers to levels of service that are "sufficient and suited to community needs." The reader must define the "sufficient" levels and then infer that they relate to effectiveness. Likewise, White (1977), in a survey of quantitative measures proposed for evaluating effectiveness, talks about "the quality of service or the value of information to the user." He does not, however, define "quality" or "value."

More recently, Lewis (1986, p. 351) states, "Developing organizational philosophies . . . will be the key to constructing effective academic libraries," but leaves the reader to make the links between philosophies and effectiveness. Kania (1988) proposes a new set of academic library standards to which specific performance measures could be appended. In measuring a library's performance against these standards, librarians are, it is implied, measuring a library's effectiveness. Hernon (1987) both exhibits and analyzes the confusion and lack of consensus about "effectiveness" in a paper urging "utility measures" rather than "performance measures" in assessing reference services. On the other hand, he does present a useful library perspective on the growing concern of some organizational researchers that researcher-imposed effectiveness criteria are not helpful to the practitioner.

The literature on libraries is not unusual in lacking a clear meaning for effectiveness. Historically, there has been little agreement in the organizational sciences, generally, about the organizational effectiveness construct. The brief review of the literature of effectiveness presented in Chapter 2 provides clear evidence of this confusion.

However, research conducted in the late 1970s and 1980s, largely by Kim Cameron and associates, has established a foundation and secured principles on which meaningful research into organizational effectiveness can now be accomplished. Cameron's critical contributions to organizational effectiveness have been to grasp and to state certain fundamental theoretical principles about effectiveness, and then to conduct research into the effectiveness of colleges and universities which is rooted in and informed by these principles.

Cameron recognized that because there is no single right way to conceptualize organizations, there is not likely to be consensus on a single correct model of organizational effectiveness. An organization's effectiveness is based on the conception its members have of that organization. He also understood that effectiveness is a construct, that is, it is something inferred from organizational behavior and not something observed directly. Accordingly, the construct "space" is unknown; one can never be sure that all relevant behaviors and their relationships have been identified and explored exhaustively. And it then follows that the best criteria for measuring effectiveness must be unknown.

Second, Cameron's research into the effectiveness of colleges and universities demonstrated that it is a multidimensional and multivariate phenomenon. That is, there are many criteria involved in effectiveness, and it is various groupings of institutional activities and processes which are effective; the effectiveness of a college or university as a whole is measured by its effectiveness in the various dimensions. Furthermore, effectiveness in one dimension may preclude effectiveness in another dimension, and it appears that individual units in higher education organizations may need to exhibit patterns of effectiveness that conflict or contradict those of other units in order for the organization as a whole to be effective.

MULTIDIMENSIONAL EFFECTIVENESS OF ACADEMIC LIBRARIES

This book applies Cameron's principles to the traditional issues of academic library effectiveness. We draw heavily on McDonald (1987), which appears to represent the first attempt to use Cameron's principles to establish a theoretical basis for studying library effectiveness. In a related study, Childers and Van House (1989), also using Cameron's principles, have similarly studied public library organizational effectiveness and, especially, its multidimensionality.

The investigation described in subsequent chapters is based on a survey of academic libraries in six Middle Atlantic states and the District of Columbia. The questionnaire asked the chief decision makers in the libraries surveyed to respond to a series of questions and statements regarding the presence, in their libraries, of a number of factors which a broad survey of library literature suggested were related to effectiveness. Their responses were analyzed using a variety of statistical procedures.

The results showed that it is possible to establish criteria for library organizational effectiveness and to design an instrument to begin to measure the phenomenon. As a construct, of course, effectiveness cannot be precisely or objectively described. However, as we will show, a properly designed and validated instrument can be used to create an imperfect but pragmatic description or approximation of this essentially subjective perception. Furthermore, as we discuss in Chapter 8, once an initial description of the phenomenon has been accomplished, batteries of objective measures can be used to generate a fine-grained analysis of its specific aspects.

The results further showed that academic library effectiveness, like that of colleges and universities, is also multidimensional and multivariate. In addition, it demonstrated that groups of academic libraries could be identified which varied together in their performance with respect to particular effectiveness dimensions.

The variables making up the dimensions, as well as the further grouping of dimensions into major domains of effectiveness, are presented and discussed in Chapter 7. The implications of these findings for library research as well as for library practice and evaluation are extensive. For example, the research raises the question whether it is possible or desirable to establish uniform standards which all academic libraries must achieve in order to be considered effective. As we point out in Chapter 5, there will always be multiple models of organizational effectiveness. The existence of such models suggests that it is unreasonable to insist that any given set of effectiveness criteria should be applied uniformly in the evaluation of library activities. Likewise, the observation that groups of libraries exist which show quite different effectiveness values for different sets of criteria (different groups of dimensions) raises the question whether their uneven performance is the result of conscious internal decisions about which activities to emphasize or is the result of poor management or external pressures. If it is the former, that is, if libraries have chosen and can justify their particular emphases, this research may suggest that the uniform application of rigorous and arbitrary standards (e.g., the Association of College and Research Libraries (ACRL) Standards) is at best irrelevant to effectiveness and, at worst, may militate against it.

Furthermore, the research revealed a significant discrepancy between the criteria users apply to evaluate a library's effectiveness (e.g., the availability of needed information on demand) and the characteristics librarians associate with effectiveness (e.g., the presence of well-developed mechanisms for access to information in remote libraries). This finding gives rise to a series of tantalizing questions. Are user expectations unreasonable, as most librarians would probably claim? Or is it possible to create local collections which could immediately satisfy most of the curriculum-related information needs of faculty and students? To what extent has the isolation which exists on many campuses of librarians from faculty contributed to largely unused collections? Have librarians been intellectually honest and professionally responsible in matching information collections to their users' needs?

Or, viewed from another perspective, are resource-sharing networks the result of large increases in the amount of needed information, or does the existence of these networks reflect parsimonious or irresponsible institutional behavior toward library funding? Is the information explosion real and important? Or, is it real, but much less significant than we have been led to believe? Has the publish-or-perish syndrome contributed extensively to academic information overload? If so, can libraries find ways to seriously discourage the process by supplying information wheat and ignoring the chaff? Should institutional administrators increase library budgets because of appeals to the relentless increase in scholarly and technical literature, or should libraries be expected to justify budget requests solidly on the basis of measured and documented curricular need? It is these and similar types of issues which the profession may be able to address concretely as it comes to a better informed understanding of effectiveness.

It is important to note the difference in perspective between the application of organizational theory to the study of library effectiveness (the approach taken in this study) and the use of a library as a setting in which to study organizational theories and practices. For example, Damanpour and Evan (1984) used a sample of eighty-four public libraries in which to apply the organizational lag model to the study of the adoption of innovation in organizations. Their concern, however, was not with libraries. Rather, their interest lay in an analysis of the effects of the rates of adoption of administrative versus technical innovations and their possible relationship to organizational effectiveness. Significantly, they cited only one library researcher and said, in effect, that although they understood his concerns about library effectiveness, these would not be addressed in their study.

In contrast, this book begins with libraries and uses organizational theory to help practitioners in academic libraries better understand their own organizations. As Cameron (1986) has noted, organizational effectiveness is mainly a problem-driven construct rather than a theory-driven construct. The issue in this book is successful libraries, not evidence for theoretical positions. Nevertheless, the hope, repeated throughout this work, is that this and similar attempts at circumscribing, describing, measuring, and testing effectiveness will lead to theory which can form an empirically defensible basis for academic library activities, a foundation they now lack.

A BRIEF NOTE ON LANGUAGE

In addition to the problem of how one defines "effectiveness," there is considerable confusion in both the information and library literature and that of the organizational sciences over the use of that word and related expressions. Words such as "goodness" and "quality" are frequently used rather loosely to mean "effectiveness," just as the terms "evaluation," "assessment," "performance measures," and "outcomes" are often used to imply its measurement. Likewise, confusion exists over expressions such as "effectiveness," "organizational effectiveness," and "organizational-level effectiveness."

As we will show, these words and expressions are not necessarily synonymous. It is important to determine exactly what a writer means by them and to distinguish carefully their connotations and nuances. For example, this book is a study of the "organizational effectiveness" of academic libraries. As such, it looks at the effectiveness of library activities as a whole, rather than the effectiveness of isolated bits and pieces of these activities which, perhaps, could be added up to some approximation of the effectiveness of the library's services. In contrast, "organizational-level effectiveness" is a technical term, used to describe the perspective from which organizational effectiveness is studied. That is, rather than studying organizational effectiveness from the perspective of selected parts of the organization, in an "organizational-level study" it is examined from the vantage point provided by the entire organization.

Similarly, with the growing attention to academic library outcomes and their measurement and assessment, there is a tendency in some of the literature to equate outcomes and effectiveness. Further confusion is generated by the use of "outcomes" (sometimes incorrectly used synonymously with "outputs") as both *indicators* of effectiveness and as *measures* of effectiveness. In this work, "effectiveness" is considered as a phenomenon present in library organizations which, as a construct, is inferred from measurable organizational behavior and attributes. But these attributes, or symptoms, are not themselves coextensive with "effectiveness." In subsequent chapters, effectiveness is discussed as a mental construct, and the differences between indicators and measures of effectiveness are analyzed.

Chapter 2

LIBRARY EFFECTIVENESS: A REVIEW

There are several ways in which the literature of effectiveness can be organized: historically; by aspect of organization studied; topically, by activity, program, or service; or by criteria chosen as either measures or indicators of effectiveness. Because of its importance for understanding the new approach to effectiveness taken in this book, the literature reviewed below has been grouped around the levels or perspectives from which organizational effectiveness has been studied: the organization as a whole (organizational-level approaches), units of the organization (suborganizational-level approaches), or the level of the individual (individual-level approaches).

ORGANIZATIONAL-LEVEL APPROACHES TO EFFECTIVENESS

The organizational sciences literature describes several models purporting to be adequate definitions of effectiveness from the perspective of the entire organization (Cameron, 1978b).

Goals

Goal accomplishment and outputs are commonly used criteria of effectiveness (Georgopolous and Tannenbaum, 1957; Etzioni, 1964; Price, 1972; Hall, 1978). In goal-based models, goal statements are used as effectiveness criteria, and the achievement of goals becomes the definition of effectiveness.

Empirical research in libraries on goal preferences and goal attainment is limited. Davis (1984) reports research into library goals based on Gross and Grambsch organizational goal theory in universities. An underlying assumption of the Davis study is that goals are appropriate and necessary indicators of effectiveness. Murphy (1987), in a wide ranging discussion of goal setting, links goal achievement to both managerial and organizational success in libraries. Hernon (1987), although not clear, seems to define library effectiveness as the degree to which goals and objectives are obtained. Van House, Weil, and McClure (1990) also define an effective library as one which achieves its goals, while acknowledging the difficulty in developing a "unified, prioritized set of goals."

Goal-based effectiveness models have been found to be useful in circumstances where the organization's goals are clear, readily measured, limited in time, and for which consensus exists among the members of the organization. However, goal accomplishment as the criterion for effectiveness has been criticized for a number of reasons. For example, an organization's official goals are not always the same as its actual or real goals. Blau and Scott (1961) point out that by concentrating on official goals there is a tendency to fail to consider the goals of the organization's constituencies or those of society at large. Merton (1957) has demonstrated that a focus on official goals may cause organizations to ignore implicit, latent, or informal goals and procedures.

Likewise, not all goals are of equal priority in theory or in practice, nor do all constituencies agree on the priorities assigned to goals. Rice (1963) has shown that the goal model cannot accommodate the varied and sometimes contradictory nature of organizational goals. In any case, priorities, even goals themselves, as criteria of effectiveness, are static entities introduced into a dynamic system. As Warner (1967) and Pfeffer (1977) point out, as the organization's behavior changes, its goals change.

Finally, in a landmark study, Lawrence and Lorsch (1969) provide significant evidence that in the goal-based model of effectiveness, the influence of the environment on the organization and its goals is not addressed. And Weick (1969) shows that organizational goals may be retrospective and be used to explain, to rationalize, or to justify organizational decisions rather than to direct them.

System Resource

Another model of effectiveness frequently found in the literature is the system resource model, or the "natural systems" approach (Yuchtman and Seashore, 1967). In this perspective the organization is judged by how well it exploits the environment to gain required resources. Efficiency is a key consideration. Euster (1986), for example, studied the "effectiveness" of forty-two university library directors in gaining the resources their organizations required. Explicitly, in the study, securing required inputs is equated with organizational success.

The system resource model of effectiveness can be appropriate when there is a demonstrable link between inputs and the performance of the organization. However, a number of concerns have been expressed about the system resource approach. Price (1972) notes the failure to distinguish efficiency and effectiveness in this model. Scott (1977) has shown that an exclusive focus on inputs may have a negative effect on outputs. Scott has also shown that the only perspective taken is that of an organization's management and that the model presupposes that the only worthwhile activities of the organization are those which are focused on inputs. Kirchoff (1977) suggests that this approach does not differ from the goal approach because, in this model, increasing inputs is the real goal of the organization. Finally, Molnar and Rogers (1976) indicate that this approach may be inappropriate for nonprofit organizations because in this type of organization inputs are not related to outputs and, therefore, inputs should not be used to judge effectiveness.

Process

A third approach or model of effectiveness is the process model, in which effectiveness is equated with internal health and well-managed internal processes and procedures (Pfeffer, 1977; Beckhard, 1969; Bennis, 1966; Likert, 1967). For example, Hershfield (1972) argues that effectiveness is a function of a library staff's ability to change their perception of what is important in libraries. Dougherty (1972) uses cost/time data from library tasks as a way of judging effectiveness. Jones (1976) maintains that effectiveness is the librarians' abilities to be creative in their interactions with materials and users. Shaughnessy (1988) argues that effectiveness is a product of the library's organizational culture. The many discussions of participative government in libraries are also examples of the process approach (e.g., Martell, 1972; Marchant, 1971).

Although the internal process model may be an appropriate one in which to assess effectiveness when there is a clear and necessary connection between processes and organizational achievement, a number of criticisms have been made of organizational processes as criteria of effectiveness. Dornbusch and Scott (1975) have shown that it is difficult to measure organizational processes, and Scott (1977) has further shown that gathering data on processes can be surprisingly costly. Haberstroh (1965) expresses concern about the accuracy of process data, and Campbell (1977) points out that this approach emphasizes means without a proper consideration of ends.

Constituency Satisfaction

Finally, a fourth major model of effectiveness is the ecological (Miles, 1980) or participant satisfaction model (Keeley, 1978). In this model, effectiveness is equated with the ability of the organization to address the needs and expectations of its strategic constituencies (Zammuto, 1982). Du Mont and Du Mont (1979) illustrate the application of this model to issues of library effectiveness, noting that Boaz (1968) suggests that a library's effectiveness must be evaluated in relation to its contribution to its host. Pings (1968) states, "Libraries . . . are man-made institutions and one reason for their existence is to support the social organizations man defines." Similarly, the various academic regional accreditation associations view library effectiveness as something which relates to how well the library supports the goals of its host institution. Several other authors (Carnovsky, 1959; DeProspo and Altman, 1972; Hamburg, Ramist, and Bommer, 1972; Salverson, 1969) also agree that library effectiveness should be defined in terms of what the library does for or contributes to its constituencies or stakeholders.

Several specific examples of the participant satisfaction model can be cited. Both DeProspo and Altman (1972) and Beasley (1968) suggest formulas to be used in measuring demand on library resources and further suggest the use of these figures in allocating the budget, designing activities, and in seeking external financial support. Orr et al. (1968a) derives a "capability index" to be used in the evaluation of a library's efficiency in delivering documents, and Trueswell (1969) investigated a library's success in meeting user requests for specific materials, at the lowest possible expense.

When an organization's stakeholders together exert considerable power or influence and the organization is obliged to respond to their demands, the strategic constituencies model of effectiveness can be useful. Nevertheless, there are three basic criticisms of the strategic constituencies model of effectiveness. Bedeian (1986) notes, first, that constituencies cannot always be trusted to have appropriate expectations for the organization and, second, that in organizations with multiple constituencies widely differing expectations are likely. Furthermore, Clark (1970) has shown that organizations can be effective regardless of conflicting or contradictory constituency expectations.

There are other models of organizational-level effectiveness encountered less frequently in the literature. Cameron (1986) lists four of them. (1) In the competing values model, an organization is effective if it is able to synthesize and meet constituency preferences. (2) The legitimacy model uses survival as a result of legitimate activity as its definition of effectiveness. (3) The absence of faults defines effectiveness in the fault-driven model, and (4) in the high performing systems model, an organization is effective if it is seen as successful in relation to other organizations. Each of these models can be useful under certain specialized circumstances, but each is insufficient by itself to explain effectiveness under all organizational conditions.

SUBORGANIZATIONAL APPROACHES TO EFFECTIVENESS

In contrast to the organizational-level approaches, the literature reveals a number of subunit- or program-level approaches to library effectiveness. Lancaster (1977) and Baker and Lancaster (1991) state that the only reasonable way to view library effectiveness is from the fragmentary, suborganizational perspective. They argue that each of the several major facets of library operations or services has to be examined independently, with the results then synthesized to present a composite picture of library effectiveness (p. 373, 1977).

Lancaster (1977, 1988) and Baker and Lancaster (1991) are the best reviews of the many suborganizational approaches to the evaluation of library services. They examine and comment on studies of catalog use, evaluations of reference service, measurement and evaluation of literature searching and information retrieval, document delivery capabilities, and collection development. They also discuss the range and scope of library services and their evaluation, and deal extensively with cost-performance-benefits considerations. However, it is important to note that the focus of their attention is on program- or subunit-level studies which, even considered collectively, would not represent an organizational-level perspective such as those discussed in the previous section.

Two aspects of library activity which have been extensively studied at the program or subunit level are the collection and the public catalog. In this next section several major collection evaluation and catalog use studies are considered, as reported by Lancaster (1977, 1988) and Baker and Lancaster (1991). These are included to illustrate the nature, scope, and range, and also the limited utility of program-specific (or suborganizational) studies in assessing or addressing total library effectiveness.

The component of library service that has probably been most subject to evaluation over the years is the collection. Lancaster organizes the various approaches to collection evaluation under two heads: quantitative and qualitative. Under the quantitative approach he places the issues of collection size and growth. For qualitative methods he lists expert judgment, bibliographies used as standards, and analysis of actual use.

Among the best known quantitative methods for evaluating an academic library collection is the application of the formula devised by Clapp and Jordan (1965). This particular method has several variants, including the formulas used by the Association of College and Research Libraries in its 1986 standards for college libraries. Regardless of the degree of refinement, the system is designed to yield the number of books a library should have when several weighted variables are added together, beginning with a base number of 50,750 volumes. These variables include the number of faculty, total number of students enrolled (with a separate category for number of honors students), and the number of undergraduate, masters, and doctoral programs offered.

Clapp and Jordan intended to show that the (minimal) adequacy of an academic library could, in fact, be measured by the number of books it contains. Their base figure of 50,750 is derived from an examination of four lists of basic books for college libraries, one of these lists dating from 1931 (Shaw). Unfortunately, there is neither theoretical nor empirical justification for their formula. The one known attempt to verify the Clapp-Jordan formula empirically was an effort by the economist McInnis (1972). He compared the results of a regression analysis on library data from graduate schools in the United States with the results of the formula and found that the regression equations produced higher figures, generally, for the expected number of volumes than those produced by the formula. Or, put another way, the Clapp-Jordan formula may provide for too low a level of adequacy.

McInnis argues that "as a very rough, quickly computed guide to minimum levels of library size," the Clapp-Jordan formula should remain as one of the measures used by librarians to suggest adequacy. But it seems questionable to us to encourage the use of a formula for which there is no theoretical or empirical justification and which puts librarians in the position of appearing to pull figures out of thin air for what could easily be construed to be self-serving reasons. In addition, these kinds of quantitative methods cannot distinguish among collections which might be of equal size but of quite different quality.

The use of expert judgment, whether in the form of a personal expert conducting an impressionistic evaluation or represented in standard or specially prepared bibliographies, appears to be a common and easily accessible method of collection evaluation. The various editions of *Books for College Libraries*, published by the American Library Association, have been used extensively to evaluate collections and to provide lists of titles for addition to collections. Other investigators (e.g., Buzzard and New, 1983) have argued that the bibliographies in faculty publications and student papers are the best criteria by which to evaluate a collection. Another approach is that advocated by Goldhor (1973, 1981). He proposes that a library's titles be checked against lists of titles appearing in reviewing media. The more frequently a title appears in such lists, presumably the more desirable it is to have. A critical variable that these methods of evaluation do not address, however, is the uniqueness of each library's users, and, presumably, the uniqueness of their information requirements.

Perhaps the most famous (or infamous) recent collection evaluation study based on an analysis of use is the Pittsburgh study (Kent, 1979). In this investigation it was found that almost 80 percent of the use of the collections in the Hillman Library of the University of Pittsburgh came from 20 percent of the collection. It was further discovered that if one applied a "use" criterion of three or more circulations for inclusion in the collection, 62 percent of the items in the collection should never have been purchased. The study generated much criticism, but a number of other studies (e.g., Ettelt, 1978; Hardesty, 1981) had findings analogous to those of the Pittsburgh investigation.

It is important to recognize, however, that "use," "recorded use," and "usefulness" are not synonymous. These distinctions are particularly important in academic libraries where the collections are likely to be lightly used unless members of the faculty create a curricular-based demand. To evaluate a collection by its use alone says very little about its potential usefulness, or effectiveness, and in any case may say nothing about the effectiveness of the library as a whole.

A second target of extensive evaluation has been the public catalog. As Lancaster identifies it, the catalog is the "single most important key to a library's collections" (1977, p. 19). And, as Gorman (1968) points out, a vital aspect of cataloging theory and practice is the use made of the catalog.

The first large-scale study of catalog use (American Library Association, 1958) attempted to identify systematically the reasons a catalog search is successful or unsuccessful. The results strongly suggest that certain well-established cataloging practices hinder the effective use of the catalog and that other cherished practices (e.g., a multiplicity of *see also* references) are largely ignored by the users. Likewise, Tagliacozzo, Rosenberg, and Kochen (1970) and Tagliacozzo and Kochen (1970) describe another major catalog use study conducted in the University of Michigan. Their findings are numerous and highly technical and address known-item searching and, to a lesser extent, subject searching. The study did identify factors influencing the effectiveness of those two types of searches.

Simultaneously with the Michigan catalog study, another was undertaken at Yale University. It is reported by Lipetz (1970, 1972). A major component of this investigation was the attempt to measure volume and distribution of catalog use, and a significant finding is that borrowing (circulation) activity can be used to predict catalog use and vice versa.

A fourth major catalog use survey was the *Requirements Study for Future Catalogues* conducted by the University of Chicago (University of Chicago, 1968) and also described by Swanson (1972). The many findings of this survey were focused specifically on an attempt to lay the foundation for the design of future catalogs. Unfortunately, automated cataloging requirements have created the need for a new set of catalog design criteria, and the full potential contribution of the Chicago study will not be realized.

There are many other smaller catalog studies (e.g., Frarey, 1953; Brooks and Kilgour, 1964). However, although these investigations may have brought about certain local improvements, such studies have not addressed the issue of the role of catalog effectiveness in overall library-use effectiveness. This has probably occurred because, to date, the emphasis has been on measuring catalog use rather than on evaluation (Lancaster, 1977). Furthermore, the catalog-use studies have generally not considered the catalog nonuser. It would seem that any full assessment of cataloging effectiveness must take into account library users who do not use the catalog.

Other areas of library service, practice, and activity that have been evaluated at the suborganizational level are

- document delivery capabilities
- reference services
- literature searching and information retrieval
- technical services
- automated systems
- human factors (personnel systems)
- cost-performance-budget interactions

Such suborganizational-level studies, however, even if added together, cannot provide an understanding of the library's overall effectiveness, because they do not include a way of assessing the strength and effect of their interactions. It is also likely, in the absence of information about the interrelatedness of various components of an academic library, that efforts to improve individual units or activities risk the possibility that overall effectiveness will be diminished in unexpected and unpredictable ways. Nevertheless, as we discuss further in subsequent chapters, once the various dimensions of effectiveness in a given library have been identified, suborganizational studies are necessary in conducting a fine-grained analysis of the elements contributing to the effectiveness of a particular dimension.

COMPOSITE OR SYNTHESIZING APPROACHES

Lancaster (1977, 1988) and Baker and Lancaster (1991) provide the best comprehensive description of the multiplicity of library measurement and evaluation studies. Significantly, they do not attempt to synthesize the studies in specific suborganizational areas, although, as has been noted above, they maintain that a complete evaluation of a library would require each area to be studied separately and then synthesized in some way to present a composite picture of library effectiveness. However, they further acknowledge that it is unlikely that it would be possible to derive a satisfactory "single figure of merit" for a library. In fact, as they point out, because each individual study would deal with completely different types of service evaluated in completely different ways, such a "single figure" would seem of dubious value.

Nevertheless, a number of composite, or synthesizing, studies appear in the literature. For example, this was attempted earlier by Rzasa and Baker (1972), who developed mathematical statements expressing a primary measure and a secondary measure of library effectiveness. The variables used to develop their "overall index of library effectiveness" were total number of items reshelved, total user population, total number who use the library, total questions asked, total questions answered satisfactorily, and the number of users in the library using their own materials or visiting for social purposes. The variables, however, were not generally accepted, and there are only two known studies which attempted to use them (Pritchard, Auckland, and Castens, 1973; Pritchard and Auckland, 1972). The equation appears to be oversimplified and does not (except for reference service) deal with failures.

Orr (1973), in a very practical discussion of library effectiveness, proposes ways to make such quantitative measures useful for measuring "the goodness of library service." However, because of the arbitrary assumptions that need to be made, the relative difficulty in applying the math, the lack of advanced mathematics training among librarians, and their apparent inability to capture every facet of library operations and services, composite quantitative measures of effectiveness are not generally used in libraries and seem unlikely to be adopted.

For example, Allen (1972) describes an attempt at the Washington State University (WSU) Library to refine into a quantitative effectiveness measure, the formula and budget model used by Washington State public colleges and universities. Data added to the model included collection age, size of reference collection, collection maintenance efforts, reference desk staffing levels, and many other measurements. An attempt was made to produce coefficients reflecting WSU library values. These were then compared to those in similar libraries. No correlations found, the model was set aside.

Likewise, a later attempt to develop a composite quantitative measure is reported by Abraham (1980). Called the "managerial rating model," it consists of five measurements resulting from the manipulation of three ratings: goal importance factor, objective importance factor, and evaluation of objective accomplishment. It was developed in the University of Washington libraries and grew out of an effort to find ways of determining the effectiveness of reference service in these libraries.

The study group assigned to this task came to the conclusion that all library activity affected reference effectiveness. It subsequently examined five major models of library effectiveness, rejected them on various grounds, and developed the "managerial rating model" which, essentially, is a way of quantifying the importance of library goals and objectives and a library's success in achieving them.

Abraham, a member of the study group, proposes that the sum of these objective effectiveness measures would give a figure expressing the effectiveness of the total library. A prototype of the model was tested, and a total library effectiveness rating was derived (but is not reported in the literature). He describes the formula, however, as a "rather tortuous mathematical exercise" and states that the model was never put into full use because of the time needed to write and evaluate goals and objectives, the unwillingness of senior staff to devote the time needed to make the model work, and the failure to discover any discernible relationships between budgets and goals and objectives.

Despite the limited usefulness and use of composite quantitative measures, librarians frequently infer effectiveness from aggregates of simple descriptive numerical data, collected by libraries on their operations, and compared to some arbitrary standard. The naive use of circulation statistics, collection size, and interlibrary loan activity in annual reports is an example of this.

LIBRARY OPERATIONS RESEARCH

Library operations research approaches to effectiveness are closely related to approaches seeking composite quantitative measures. Although operations research techniques are highly quantitative, they involve much more than merely deriving composite quantitative measures. Central to operations research is the mathematical model which, to a greater or lesser extent, represents elements of a system's behavior. Presumably the model describes the behavior of the system under study, and from the model a solution to a problem or set of problems is derived. The model and the solution(s) are tested, controls over the solution are established, and the solution is implemented. All of this leads, ideally, to an effective system.

Two well-known operations research efforts are represented by Morse (1968) and Raffel and Shishko (1969). These monographs are based on the attempts made to apply formal systems analysis and operations research to management problems in the libraries of the Massachusetts Institute of Technology during the middle and late 1960s. Morse used statistics of past circulation to develop models which can predict future demand for books. Raffel and Shishko examined "weeding" criteria models with a view to their cost and effectiveness (that is, what is the best and cheapest way to retire portions of a very large science collection).

Morse (1968) is perhaps the best known early leader in library operations research. However, Leimkuhler (Leimkuhler and Cox, 1964) is another early proponent of library operations research and is especially associated with collection evaluation and evaluation of document delivery capabilities (Leimkuhler, 1967, 1969; Leimkuhler and Cooper, 1971).

Hamburg (1974) represents one of the best known efforts to design and develop a model for a library statistical information system. This model was intended to be a comprehensive and flexible framework for planning and decision making by library administrators. A significant criterion of effectiveness in this model was the item-use day of library materials. As with many other criteria, however, no support has been developed in the profession for this concept as an indicator of library effectiveness.

While the application of operations research to libraries has led to an improved understanding of both libraries and library users (O'Neill, 1984), its contribution to an understanding of effectiveness appears to be very limited. O'Neill notes that operations research has developed a unique vocabulary and suggests that this has presented an important obstacle to individuals without an extensive mathematical background. Leimkuhler (1979) and Buckland (1978) also point out the very limited ability of operations research to address the large issues of effectiveness, not only because of the complexity of the mathematical models, but also because of its cost (which can be prohibitive for small libraries) and because of the arbitrary, unverified assumptions that such research involves.

The more critical difficulty with applying operations research to the question of library effectiveness is perhaps the lack of adequate definition (O'Neill, 1984). As he notes, if operations research lacks a satisfactory definition, it should not be surprising that library operations research also lacks an acceptable definition.

Furthermore, while operations research can identify how something should be done, it cannot identify what should be done. O'Neill (1984, pp. 518–519) puts library operations research in perspective:

> There are many ways to measure the service provided by libraries. There is the quality of the service, the quantity of the service, and the value of the service. There is not, however, an accepted way to estimate value. Should the value be based on how much good the service does? Should it be based on the market value; that is, how much someone is willing to pay for it? Most successful applications of operations research have involved systems where there was broad acceptance of the objective of the system and suitable measures to evaluate the outcome. In business applications, the objectives are usually straightforward. Frequently, as in the newsboy problem, the objective is as simple as maximizing the profit. It should not be surprising that, if there is not agreement on the objective, there will not be agreement on the solution.

In recent years, operations research has lost most of its distinctiveness, and is now largely associated with other quantitative methods. In the 1970s, several very well received and popular monographs on the subject appeared

(Buckland, 1975; Brophy, Ford, Hindle, and MacKenzie, 1972; Chen, 1976). However, in the same decade "bibliometrics" was becoming the term to describe the kind of quantitative research conducted on libraries, even though bibliometrics encompasses considerably more than mere operations research (e.g., probability and statistics, information retrieval, citation analysis, and computing). In 1981, the American Library Association published a work on operations research (Rowley and Rowley, 1981), but in the ensuing ten years very little on the subject has appeared. Recently, Kraft and Boyce (1991) published their *Operations Research for Libraries and Information Agencies*, and acknowledged that "the use of operations research techniques in libraries [may] have slowed considerably" (p. 24). They note this with some regret because, as they observe, software packages now make the necessary algorithms available, and it is no longer necessary to understand their complexities. However, there does not appear to be much enthusiasm for the reintroduction of operations research into library management.

CONCLUSION

What observations or conclusions can be drawn from a review of the organizational effectiveness literature? Why are there so many different and confusing or conflicting ways to define and measure what is generally recognized to be the central concern of any organization—its success? And why do librarians appear unable to agree on the meaning and measurement of the effectiveness of their organizations? Academic librarianship would appear to be an exceedingly homogeneous occupation, in which practitioners and organizations are held together very tightly in a web of common agreements and understandings. For example, consider the disintegration of libraries which would occur if only two institutions were to fold: OCLC, Inc. and the Library of Congress. Shouldn't a common culture and technical system lead to a common understanding of effectiveness?

As we discuss later in the book, conflicting models of effectiveness exist because no one knows how broad an area organizational effectiveness covers. Different models capture different aspects of effectiveness, but none, by itself, is sufficient to describe the totality of effectiveness. But humans, it seems, have a low tolerance, generally, for ambiguity and, with respect to the ambiguity of organizational effectiveness, respond in one of two ways. They either ignore the matter (or treat it trivially) or insist that their particular insight and understanding is sufficient or comprehensive.

With respect to many libraries and librarians, however, there seems to have been, until rather recently, a considerable working consensus on the appropriate model for academic library effectiveness. Simply put, it is "more is necessarily better," or the system resource model. As most, if not all, library managers will admit, more money is always better and less money is always worse. All other considerations are subordinate to, and controlled by, the budget. More money means more books and journals, and the more of these the library has, the better, presumably, it is. See, for example, the annual rankings of research libraries by the Association of Research Libraries. The use of these rankings to suggest that bigger is better has been roundly criticized by Dougherty (1991, p. A32). "Libraries," he states, "should gauge their quality not in terms of size but in terms of how successful library users are in obtaining the information they want and whether librarians can obtain and deliver documents and information in a *timely* manner. . . . For most library users, success is getting your hands on what you need, when you need it."

Some might argue that the growing concerns in academic libraries with outputs and outcomes reveal a shift away from an unfashionable concern with inputs. But commonsense judgment suggests that a library's success in gaining needed resources will always be a mark of its effectiveness. It is true that somewhere, somehow, the eyes and ears of those who need academic information have to meet the pages, screens, and speakers of acquired information resources. But the question raised by the literature review is whether the library's ability to gain resources is a sufficient single measure of its effectiveness and, if not, where it fits in an evaluation of a library's performance. And if resource inputs are not a sufficient explanation for a library's "goodness," what other considerations are there? These questions are addressed in Chapters 3, 4, and 5. In Chapters 6 and 7, we discuss a way of testing possible answers to these questions, and in Chapters 8 and 9, we discuss the implications of what we found.

Chapter 3

LIBRARY EFFECTIVENESS: A NEW APPROACH

The review of the literature suggests that there probably is no one best approach to the study of organizational effectiveness. Thus, it is not surprising that there should be strong negative reactions to effectiveness studies. Campbell (1977) talks about the "helter-skelter" nature of effectiveness literature which displays the underlying lack of coherence and theory in effectiveness studies and then, addressing the issue of research, states that while the record shows some success, it also shows much heartache and would not overwhelm an investigator with optimism. Goodman (1979) goes even further, suggesting that a moratorium be called on all studies of organizational effectiveness, as well as on all chapters and books on organizational effectiveness. But one of the most damaging statements comes from Cameron and Whetten (1983, p. 1):

> In the past two decades, at least seven books have been produced on the subject of organizational effectiveness.... Without exception, each begins by pointing out the conceptual disarray and methodological ambiguity surrounding this construct. In addition, several hundred articles and book chapters have been written in that period..., and almost all acknowledge that little agreement exists regarding what organizational effectiveness means or how properly to assess it. Unfortunately, this plethora of writing and research has failed to produce a meaningful definition of organizational effectiveness, let alone a theory of effectiveness. The writing has been fragmented, noncumulative, and frequently downright confusing.

However, a significant breakthrough in the conceptualization and research of organizational effectiveness appears to have been made by Cameron (1978a,b). His research, discussed in detail in the next chapter, recognizes the subjective (and contradictory) nature of effectiveness, eschews univariate measures of effectiveness in favor of multivariate and dimensionalized ones, argues for testing a comprehensive set of effectiveness criteria rather than an exhaustive set which, presumably, could never be known, and attempts to map out the geography of effectiveness so that subsequent detailed analysis can proceed.

Cameron's approach has been recognized by Cummings (1982) as making a significant contribution to the "researchableness" of organizational effectiveness. Cummings points out that at a time when major reviews of the organizational effectiveness literature were calling for a closer connection between theory, operational definitions, and research methods as well as for longitudinal designs examining the determinants of effectiveness across organizations, Cameron was already making significant progress. In fact, Cummings identifies Cameron's work as "most impressive in this regard" (p. 563), noting that not only has Cameron empirically examined the dimensions of effectiveness of universities and colleges, but also has both built and tested theory concerning the determinants of effectiveness within this domain.

The usefulness of Cameron's approach is demonstrated in his own research into the effectiveness of colleges and universities (Cameron, 1978a, b; Cameron and Tschirhart, 1992), and in other research based on some or all of his approaches to effectiveness (e.g., Martin, Lewis, and Serey, 1985; Edwards, Faerman, and McGrath, 1986). And the developing consensus on the proper meaning and study of organizational effectiveness among organizational researchers, discussed in Chapter 4, is due in large part to the work of Cameron in the late 1970s and 1980s.

Cameron's success suggests that his approach is viable and can be accepted, for sound empirical reasons, as a method by which to measure library effectiveness. As will be shown below, library organizational effectiveness research needs to begin organizing a systematic approach to the construct and to make an attempt to build theory with reference to other related work. As in organizational studies, generally, different attempts to map the library effectiveness terrain have mostly been recorded with no consideration given to how they relate to one another. Isolated evaluations have been the rule, and individual efforts have generally been offered as replacements, rather than extensions, of earlier work. Likewise, while some efforts have been too broad to provide much real understanding, others have been too focused on limited issues to be useful in the evaluation of the library as a whole. While it is true that multiple perspectives (models) are required to understand effectiveness, the results of these multiple perspectives must always be considered in relationship to one another. As Cameron and Whetten point out, it is only in this manner that "a cumulative literature mapping this construct space can be developed" (1983, p. 20).

Support for an integrative approach to library effectiveness comes in a major review of the criteria used to measure effectiveness completed by Evans, Borko, and Ferguson (1972). They begin by noting the severe problem of the literature's failure to distinguish between criteria and measures of those criteria. Their solution is to deduce six "criterion concepts" from the literature—accessibility, cost, user satisfaction, response time, cost/benefit ratio, use—and then to group thirty-two "criterion measures" under the appropriate "concepts" (e.g., staff size, staff skills and characteristics, unit costs, ratio of documents circulated to various classes of users, ratio of services provided to total cost, etc.).

Evans, Borko, and Ferguson also note several problems in measuring library performance. They maintain that although there may be many possible methods of measurement, an examination of the literature shows that libraries have tended to employ a multiplicity of variations on a few basic approaches. Furthermore, most studies concentrate on only one or two library services, without considering the total service program or the need to use multiple criteria for evaluating services. These studies also generally fail to recognize the importance of weighting the various criteria assumed to be contributing to effectiveness.

Finally, these authors suggest that researchers interested in library effectiveness should expend less effort developing modifications of existing measures of performance evaluation and invest more energy into developing precise operational procedures in which (1) the variables involved in the measurement of each of their criterion concepts would be defined; (2) the statistical data and formulas needed to calculate the criterion measures would be specified; (3) steps which would allow these individual criterion measures to be combined in an evaluation of total library performance would be identified; and (4) a rationale for weighting the individual criterion measures would be established. Ideally, researchers would eventually arrive at a procedure whereby meaningful comparisons could be made of libraries.

Further support for an integrative approach to library effectiveness is found in Du Mont and Du Mont (1979) and Du Mont (1980). In a major review of library effectiveness to date, Du Mont and Du Mont describe four major approaches to viewing library effectiveness, including (1) those which emphasize physical input (e.g., number of staff, budget); (2) those which emphasize the organizational dynamics of the library (e.g., the relationship between the library staff and the formal library organization); (3) those which emphasize library outputs (e.g., materials and services) as perceived by patrons; and (4) those which emphasize library outcomes (e.g., materials and services) as they affect elements within the society as a whole.

The Du Mont and Du Mont outline powerfully illustrates the compartmentalization of approaches to library effectiveness. For example, they show that approaches which focus on library inputs tend to be limited to studies of library facilities, services, and the staff needed to provide those services, and seem to be based on the argument that levels of input in these areas are an important way in which librarians can compare their accomplishments with those of others and can successfully pressure authorities into increasing funding. In contrast, approaches which emphasize the organizational dynamics of the library focus on understanding and improving staff motivation and management styles, though they may fail to address the influence library inputs have on personnel interactions or the relationship between a library's internal climate and its effectiveness as perceived by the user. Finally, investigations which evaluate the library's interaction with users as a measure of effectiveness (e.g., many "output" approaches), or which attempt to describe the effect of library services on society (e.g., many "outcomes" approaches), do recognize that, in the end, the purpose of the library is service. But they also risk emphasizing immediate user satisfaction to the possible detriment of long-term library development and even long-term user benefits.

Underlying each of these approaches is the assumption that the aspect of library organization or service being studied is directly and necessarily related to effectiveness and, thus, becomes a measurement of that effectiveness. As Du Mont and Du Mont argue, however, the isolation and independent measurement of one or another aspect does not allow the interaction of these elements to be considered, and, thus, does not allow the library to be viewed as a whole, an "entity in its own right." Instead, an integrative approach would seem more appropriate. Such an approach would, "through the unification of all perspectives," lead to "one conceptual vision of library effectivenesses" (p. 130).

The Du Mont study and the Evans, Borko, and Ferguson review illustrate the efforts some librarians have made to try to establish an integrative approach to effectiveness, using multiple criteria. In the next section the approach taken in this study is explored.

STATEMENT OF THE PROBLEM AND RESEARCH APPROACH

The research reported in this book addresses itself to three major questions:

1. Is it possible to establish criteria for assessing academic library organizational effectiveness and to develop an instrument that will measure library effectiveness?
2. Can dimensions of academic library organizational effectiveness be identified?

3. Can groups of academic libraries be identified which show high effectiveness in contrast with others which show lower effectiveness?

There are three broad reasons why we undertook this exploratory research. The first is the interest of the library and information-handling profession in library effectiveness and its seeming inability to come to terms with it, successfully. As we have noted, most, if not all, authors and investigators in library effectiveness offer significantly restricted definitions, discussions, and research on the topic, and present proposals and conclusions that are noncumulative, usually not generalizable, and mostly noncomparable.

This inability to come to terms with the breadth and depth of library effectiveness reflects the general state of disarray in the field of effectiveness studies. With the work of the investigators discussed above, this disarray is beginning to be ordered and organized, making "effectiveness" a truly researchable subject. Perhaps it is unfair, then, to be severely critical of the state of the profession's knowledge of library effectiveness. Nevertheless, it is also important to note that most writing and most of what little empirical research exists on library effectiveness ignores the very considerable body of scholarship on organizational effectiveness. And yet, is there a librarian or library manager who will not invoke "effectiveness" as the final, unassailable criterion of the worth of his or her program, service, or organization? Buckland (1983, p. 195) captures a good deal of the dilemma in the following:

> Although the quest for the Grail of Library Goodness has not (yet) been successful, there has been no lack of measures of performance proposed, nor of people proposing them. There have been plenty of suggestions. What is lacking is a sense of coherence—a sense of fitting together to form a whole. It is noticeable that the numerous empirical efforts need to be counterbalanced by a greater attention to theory, to context, and to how the bits and pieces fit together.

In what follows, we concentrate on academic libraries, but believe that the same principles and approach would also be suitable for other kinds of libraries.

Second, the pioneering work of Cameron provides a promising basis for studying the relationship between college and library organizational effectiveness. Libraries do not exist in a vacuum. Presumably, the *mere* acquisition of materials and operations upon these materials (such as cataloging and inventory control) cannot be justified in an academic setting. Libraries are assumed to exist for purposes related to the purposes of a college or university. If that is so, then one should be able to posit a relationship or a set or sets of relationships between the effectiveness of the university and its library.

Even the casual observer can note what appears to be an involvement of the library in the teaching and research processes of the university. Librarians are frequently quoted as desiring to make their libraries an integral part of those processes. Is there then a relationship between the effectiveness of a library and that of its host institution? Is the effectiveness of either an independent variable on which the other's effectiveness depends, if only in part?

Embedded in the second issue is an assumption frequently made, namely, that library effectiveness is a function of the degree to which the library is integrated with the college or university's teaching and research (Johnson, 1939; Branscomb, 1940; Carlson, 1946; Battin, 1984; Brown, 1984). This has never been demonstrated empirically. Given the failure of the Monteith College Library experiment (Knapp, 1966) and the library-college movement (Hopkins, 1981), and our growing insight into the "loosely coupled" nature of the parts comprising institutions of higher education (Weick, 1976), there is increased recognition that the relationship of the library to its host is quite complex and varies in what appear to be, superficially, unpredictable ways.

The library-college movement, begun by Louis Shores in 1934, was an attempt to establish instructional patterns in colleges in which librarians would become teachers, working in partnership with subject-specialist professors, to direct students in independent, interdisciplinary study. Thirty years later, Patricia Knapp tested a modified version of the library-college idea in Monteith College, an undergraduate component of Wayne State University. In this experiment students were instructed in library search procedures to solve information problems arising from their course work. In addition, they were involved in small group discussions in which librarians helped them to fit their information-searching experiences into a broader library/information system context.

There are many reasons why neither the library-college nor the Monteith College Library experiment succeeded, a discussion of which is beyond the purposes of this book. Two reasons, however, deserve comment. For either to have succeeded, both librarians and teaching faculty would have had to be in very different places with respect to their training and professional preoccupations. In the end, librarians were not teachers, and teaching faculty, as Knapp makes clear, were not about to adopt far-reaching innovations in their classrooms, certainly not innovations proposed by librarians, of all people.

On the other hand, a good argument can be made for both the library-college movement and the Monteith College Library experiment as important and necessary, if premature, forebears of the present large interest in bibliographic instruction and information-seeking skills development, generally. The success of the integrated bibliographic instruction in Earlham College, the success of librarians as teachers in Sangamon State University, the present concern for information literacy (e.g., Breivik and Gee, 1989), and the successful development and testing of a syllabus-integrated collection development method (McDonald and Micikas, 1990) argue that there may be sound academic and pedagogical reasons for the integration of the library with an institution's learning and teaching environment. This relationship and the question of the degree of "coupling" is discussed in detail in Chapter 5.

College and university effectiveness has been measured and predicted by Cameron, from 1978 onward in an ongoing longitudinal study (Cameron, 1978a,b; Cameron and Tschirhart, 1992). If library effectiveness can be measured successfully and predicted in ways that are comparable with Cameron's research, it would seem that a basis could be established for examining the relationship between a library's effectiveness and that of its host institution. Accordingly, we need to measure library effectiveness in ways that will enable future investigators to predict effectiveness and subsequently to compare library with college organizational effectiveness.

Finally, we need to begin a process in which the academic library user—students and members of the faculty—would be the ultimate beneficiary. Regardless of how one might recognize or build an effective library, most librarians would maintain, *a priori*, that such a library must be one which benefits its users. Although users may have contradictory expectations, an effective library, then, must be one which benefits as many of its constituencies as possible, even in ways or with activities and practices which may not ever be apparent to users.

Contemporary American academic library services, however, in their evolution from simple beginnings in nineteenth-century colleges and academies, have been modelled largely on the public library (Shiflett, 1981). Practices and activities have generally been introduced and developed with a growing concern for users but with little empirical evidence as to the effects these might have on them. One result of this has been that users, especially student users in research libraries, may not be well served (Miksa, 1989). Although librarians have struggled with issues of assessment, they have been largely unsuccessful at measuring effectiveness as a whole, and thus are faced with the problem that if they cannot recognize effectiveness, they are unlikely to implement changes that could unambiguously lead to improved effectiveness.

This is not to say that libraries cannot make a range of pragmatic changes which improve individual functions within the organization. There is no doubt that some of these changes increase a library's organizational effectiveness. As has been noted, however, attempts to improve a single unit or service or activity in isolation from other such entities, because they ignore the interactions which generate benefits to users, may not lead to increased effectiveness and could, from ignorance, lead to less effective library organizations. Progress has been made in finding ways to measure and improve the effectiveness of bits and pieces of library service. What is critically needed is comparable progress in understanding, assessing, and measuring the effectiveness of library service as a whole.

Chapter 4

ASSESSING ORGANIZATIONAL EFFECTIVENESS

In the past decade, largely as a result of Cameron's research and writing, a consensus in the meaning and significance of organizational effectiveness has emerged. Areas of disagreement remain, of course, but the sense is of writers and researchers agreeing to disagree on these issues, rather than engaging in counterproductive attacks on the legitimacy of another's assumptions and approaches. The five major areas of consensual agreement and the three major areas of continuing conflict are discussed below.

Reflecting these areas of agreement and disagreement, Cameron's approach to measuring and predicting effectiveness in colleges and universities incorporates several fundamental principles of organizational-level effectiveness research. Because of the relationship between Cameron's work and the research described here, these principles and the broad design of Cameron's research are also presented and discussed below. We note the importance of effectiveness as a construct and pay particular attention to the most basic of Cameron's assessment principles, the definition and specification of the organizational domain whose effectiveness is being assessed. Finally, we discuss three key issues involved in the application of Cameron's principles to library effectiveness research.

CONSENSUS IN ORGANIZATIONAL EFFECTIVENESS

Cameron (1986) notes five areas or five themes that typically now appear in most writing about organizational effectiveness (pp. 540–541):

1. Despite the ambiguity and confusion surrounding it, the construct of organizational effectiveness is central to the organizational sciences and cannot be ignored in theory and research.

2. Because no conceptualization of an organization is comprehensive, no conceptualization of an effective organization is comprehensive. As the metaphor describing an organization changes, so does the definition or appropriate model of organizational effectiveness.
3. Consensus regarding the best, or [at least, a] sufficient, set of indicators of effectiveness is impossible to obtain. Criteria are based on the values and preferences of individuals, and no specifiable construct boundaries exist.
4. Different models of effectiveness are useful for research in different circumstances. Their usefulness depends on the purposes and constraints placed on the organizational effectiveness investigation.
5. Organizational effectiveness is mainly a problem-driven construct rather than a theory-driven construct.

Cameron also notes three areas of continuing conflict and disagreement (1986, pp. 543–544):

1. Evaluators of effectiveness often select models and criteria arbitrarily in their assessments, relying primarily on convenience.
2. Indicators of effectiveness selected by researchers are often too narrowly or too broadly defined, or they do not relate to organizational performance.
3. Outcomes are the dominant type of criteria used to assess effectiveness by researchers, whereas effects are most frequently used in policy decisions and by the public. [Cameron illustrates the difference between "outcomes" and "effects" from the tobacco industry. In the 1970s, tobacco firms were highly profitable and productive, that is, had desirable "outcomes," even though their "outputs," cigarettes, had, in their carcinogenic properties, highly undesirable "effects."]

In this chapter and the next the implications of this consensus and continuing disagreement will be discussed, in relation to library effectiveness. First, organizational effectiveness is a mental *construct*. As such, there is no single indicator which can be used to operationalize it (Campbell, 1977). A mental construct cannot be observed, pinpointed, weighed, or otherwise measured directly. Like love, justice, anger, patriotism, or relevance, organizational effectiveness has no objective basis in reality (Kaplan, 1964). Instead, it is an abstraction that is used to give meaning to the *idea* of effectiveness. Although a construct may lack an objective reality, this does not mean that every individual defines it differently. Constructs emerge (or are given names) when social groups share and then struggle to articulate common understandings. For a construct to have any significance, there must be a shared understanding of its core meaning, even though there may be considerable disagreement about the extent of the construct or its proper application.

Furthermore, as a construct, organizational effectiveness is composed of many different *dimensions* and, as Cameron (1978b, pp. 3–4) points out:

> The dimensions of organizational effectiveness are *mutable* (composed of different criteria at different life stages), *comprehensive* (including a multiplicity of dimensions), *divergent* (relating to different constituencies), *transpositive* (altering relevant criteria when different levels of analysis are used), and *complex* (having nonparsimonious relationships among dimensions).

That is, organizations can seek many and contradictory goals (Warner, 1967; Perrow, 1970; Hall, 1972, 1978; Dubin, 1976); effectiveness criteria can change as an organization moves through time (Yuchtman and Seashore, 1967; Kimberly, 1976a; Miles and Cameron, 1982); the various constituencies of an organization may be significant at certain times but not at others, or with respect to only particular organizational elements (Friedlander and Pickle, 1968; Barney, 1977; Scott, 1977); criteria change from one level of the organization to another (Price, 1972; Weick, 1977); and it can be impossible to determine the relationships between the various dimensions of effectiveness in an organization (Seashore, Indik, and Georgopolous, 1960; Mahoney and Weitzel, 1969; Kirchoff, 1975, 1977).

DOMAINS OF ORGANIZATIONAL EFFECTIVENESS

Cameron defines *organizational effectiveness* as "*successful organizational transactions*." "Organizational transactions" refers to any activities involving the interaction of people or units or both within the organization. As Cameron argues (1978b, p. 17), this definition suggests a broader scope than goal attainment, emphasis on input acquisition, a state of "organizational health," or strategic constituencies consensus, the four major definitions used in the literature, and it assumes an organizational context. Individual, suborganizational, or environmental transactions which have an impact on the organization are subsumed within it.

This broad conceptual definition of organizational effectiveness as "successful organizational transactions," however appropriate it may be in theory, is difficult to apply in practice. As Cameron points out, "the assessment of effectiveness must always be made in relation to certain constituencies or sources (*someone* must determine what 'successful' means) and [in relation to] certain organizational aspects" (Cameron, 1978b, p. 18).

Because of this, Cameron maintains that the analysis of organizational effectiveness can only proceed after the domains being assessed are defined and specified. These domains identify the types of organizational trans-

Table 4–1
Organizational Effectiveness Domains

Levels of Analysis	Organizational Aspects: INPUTS	PROCESSES	OUTPUTS
INDIVIDUALS	Individual Resource Acquisition	Individual "Health"	Individual Productivity
SUBUNITS	Subunit Resource Acquisition	Subunit "Health"	Subunit Productivity
ORGANIZATION	Organizational Resource Acquisition	Organizational "Health"	Organizational Productivity

(from Cameron, 1978 B, p.19)

actions which are used in an effectiveness study. He notes a number of possible organizational domains shown on Table 4–1.

The table identifies three levels at which a study of an organization could be focused (individual, subunit, or organizational) and three organizational aspects which would need to be considered (inputs, processes, outputs). Each cell (each intersection of a particular aspect with a particular level) represents a single domain.

The various aspects of the organization are represented by the vertical columns. For example, the first cell on the bottom row, Organizational Resource Acquisition, refers to approaches which define effectiveness as securing required organizational inputs. Yuchtman and Seashore (1967) illustrate this type of approach. The next cell, Organizational "Health," encompasses models "which focus on the normative procedures or practices found in an organization" (p. 20). For example, Clark (1962) holds that organizational effectiveness is derived from organizational behaviors which maintain the status quo and growth. Bennis (1966), Miles (1965), and Steers (1977) likewise fit into this cell. And, finally, as Cameron explains, the third cell, Organizational Productivity, includes studies which emphasize goal attainment and outcomes. "Productivity" is used in a broader sense than the efficiency ratio which relates the value of outputs to the value of inputs (Lupton, 1976). Instead, "productivity" in the output cells has to do with the production of "effects" or outputs or results as seen in work by Price (1968), Duncan (1973), and Child (1974a, 1975).

Three different levels of analyses of the organizational aspects are possible (individual, subunit, organizational). For example, cell one, Individual Resource Acquisition, refers to an individual's efforts in bringing resources into the organization as a criterion for effectiveness. The second cell, Individual "Health," refers to individual and interpersonal processes. Argyris (1962) argues that feelings of self-worth and interpersonal relationships are critical for effectiveness, and Likert (1967) maintains that the effective organization is one where individuals have full participation in decision making. The third cell, Individual Productivity, recognizes that individual outputs and performance criteria are central to the effectiveness construct (Lawler, Hall, and Oldham, 1974; Macy and Mirvis, 1976; March and Mannari, 1976). This refers to the services and tasks which the individuals perform within the context of the organization.

Perhaps a better understanding of the differences among these levels of analysis can be obtained by comparing one organizational aspect down the levels. As has already been noted, Individual "Health" refers to individual and interpersonal processes and incorporates ideas of participation in decision making, maintaining feelings of self-worth, and providing for effective interpersonal relationships. Similarly, Subunit "Health" incorporates the idea of effective interunit interactions, that is, effective coordination of activities among the units of an organization. Finally, as we have also already noted, Organizational "Health" refers to homeostatic models of effectiveness. Such models emphasize stability, continuity, normality, and have to do with organizational mechanisms that are self-monitoring and self-correcting.

If it is true, as Cameron argues, that the assessment of effectiveness must be made in relation to certain constituencies or sources and in relation to certain organizational aspects and levels, that is, that the analysis can only proceed after the domains being assessed are defined and specified, then it is important to understand these organizational domains in a library context. The following list contains examples of what a library might do if it wished to improve its effectiveness in any of the nine domains charted on Table 4–1.

Individual Resource Acquisition: Hire an assistant director with a consistent record of attracting grant and other extramural funding; retain as director an individual who every year is able to secure significant increases in the library's operating budget.

Individual "Health": Introduce "quality circles" into the technical services department; locate recommendations or decisions concerning staff appointments, evaluations, term renewals, and dismissals in a personnel committee of peers.

Individual Productivity: Evaluate each reference librarian's database-searching ability and design additional learning experiences suited to each one's specific needs.

Subunit Resource Acquisition: Encourage the public services department to negotiate the delivery of more online products and computer equipment from the systems department.

Subunit "Health": Require the processing department to determine with the circulation department how many new books it will send each day to be shelved; require the systems department to negotiate with the reference department the appropriate time of day for maintenance work in the online catalog.

Subunit Productivity: Increase the number of titles accurately cataloged each day; add subject specialists to the reference staff.

Organizational Resource Acquisition: Increase the number of books added annually to the collection.

Organizational "Health": Write and enforce a library policies and procedures manual.

Organizational Productivity: Establish a set of library goals and objectives and direct all activity to meeting them.

Cameron's classification scheme for the domains of an organization carries with it several important implications (1978b, p. 24):

- Effectiveness in one domain may not relate to effectiveness in another domain.
- It would appear that any study of organizational effectiveness should operationalize the construct in terms of a particular domain or set of domains so that different organizational aspects and levels can be understood.
- The particular domain chosen by a researcher may not be as important as it is that the domain be recognized and specified.

A single effectiveness study can (and, perhaps, must) encompass each of the three organizational aspects (inputs, processes, outputs). However, to avoid an elaboration of possibly contradictory perspectives, it can realistically be focused at only one level of analysis (individual, subunit, or organizational) at a time. Effectiveness at one level may relate differently to the variables than effectiveness at another level.

Here we are primarily concerned with the overall, organizational level, which is, in the end, what really matters most. The argument can be expressed quite succinctly: only when the individual serves as a representative of the organization or when generalizations to the organization can be made based on subunit criteria, are these levels appropriately used in an investigation of the effectiveness of an organization as a whole.

Thus, Cameron operationalizes organizational effectiveness as a concern with three organizational aspects—inputs, processes, and outputs—at the *organizational* level. Cameron states (1978b, p. 26):

> These three cells were selected not because they are more appropriate than the others, but because they help address certain methodological issues arising from the nature of colleges and universities as organizations. Based on this operationalization, *institutions of higher education are effective to the extent to which they produce valued and desired outcomes, maintain organizational ability and vitality, and acquire needed resources without destroying the environment.* (emphasis is Cameron's)

Cameron also notes that such an approach is a comprehensive one, capturing the essence of a significant variety of effectiveness definitions proposed in the literature.

LIBRARY ORGANIZATIONAL-LEVEL RESEARCH

The following section discusses and defends the application of Cameron's principles to the study of library effectiveness. The first issue examined is the appropriateness of treating the academic library as a separate organization, rather than as a subunit of the college or university. Khandwalla (1977) states that so long as one clearly defines the unit to be studied and that unit exhibits all the attributes of an organization, such an approach is legitimate. In fact, he goes on to argue that organization theory is designed to explain the behavior of all such units, be they small or large, embedded or independent entities.

According to Khandwalla, the essential properties of an organization are (1) hierarchy of authority; (2) rules, procedures, controls, and techniques; (3) formality of communication; (4) specialization of functions and division of labor; (5) employment of skilled personnel; and (6) specificity of purpose. Clearly, academic libraries possess all the requisite properties.

The second issue relates to how Cameron's three key organizational aspects (inputs, processes, and outputs) are applicable to libraries. To be effective, organizations must bring in resources from the environment (inputs). In the library, librarians and users, for example, are resources which the organization uses as building blocks for academic programs and activities, and as raw materials in the service process. Likewise, in effective organizations processes are both "viable" and "vital." "Viability" refers to internal processes and practices in an organization. "Vitality" refers to the long-term survival of the organization. In this study, the viability and vitality of a number of internal library processes are examined, including administrative policies and procedures and professional and clerical staff activities.

Finally, effective organizations generate valued and desired outcomes. Cameron defines "valued" outcomes as "those outcomes to which the external environment is receptive or which it considers important" (1978b, p. 26). For this study, the external environment is considered to be both the college or university and the information-handling environment with which a library has transactions: network systems, consortia, professional associations, and so forth. Valued outcomes, then, are those which are perceived to be important by students, faculty, administrators, the external professional culture, and society at large. In contrast, "desired" outcomes are defined as those which "refer to internal goal accomplishment or to those outcomes internally valued in the organization" and have to do with the objectives and expectations of librarians and staff (1978b, p. 26).

The third issue relates to the definition of library organizational effectiveness. To assure comparability with Cameron's study, we have defined effectiveness as successful organizational transactions. These transactions include the interaction among all activities and people in the library, as well as those transactions between the library and its environment.

Chapter 5

CRITERIA FOR ASSESSING ACADEMIC LIBRARY ORGANIZATIONAL EFFECTIVENESS

The choice of criteria for assessing organizational effectiveness depends on a variety of organizational and theoretical factors which collectively form a perspective on the organization to be studied and suggest the appropriate research approach. The following discussion is intended to describe the theoretical perspective which guided the selection of criteria in the present study.

MULTIPLE MODELS OF EFFECTIVENESS

It is not likely that universally acceptable causal relationships between a set of predictor variables and "effectiveness" will ever be identified because the meaning of the dependent variable (effectiveness) is different, depending on which model of organizational effectiveness is being used. For example, a possible predictor variable in the goal model of organizational success might be the degree of clarity in the goal statements. In contrast, in the resource acquisition model of effectiveness, the degree of clarity of the goal statements is largely irrelevant since effectiveness is defined differently in this model.

Moreover, multiple models of organizational effectiveness will always exist, and there appear to be three reasons why, as suggested by Cameron and Whetten (1983).

1. *Multiple models of organizational effectiveness are products of multiple, arbitrary models of organizations.* There is no consensus in the organizational sciences on the right way to conceptualize organizations. One reason for this is that the merit of conceptualizations depends on their thoroughness (i.e., if they emphasize phenomena ignored in other models)

rather than their accuracy. So far, it appears that no concept has mapped all the appropriate phenomena.

Different models of effectiveness, then, follow from different models of organizations, and their uniqueness has to do with differing foci, not with the relative advantages of one model over the other. Consequently, the criteria of effectiveness emphasized in a given organization depend on the conceptualization accepted there.

2. *The construct space of organizational effectiveness is unknown*. Effectiveness, like justice, intelligence, motivation, and relevance, is a construct and, thus, a subjective, mental image. Constructs are inferred from observable human behavior; they cannot be discovered or defined by observing individual events. Cameron and Whetten assert "as a construct, the total meaning of effectiveness is unknown" (p. 7), and the various models of effectiveness (e.g., goal model or system resource model) do not capture or map the total construct space. Although each has its own value, none is thorough enough to supplant other models.

Cameron and Whetten illustrate the problem succinctly and very much to the purposes of this research (1983, p. 8):

> This lack of mapping of the construct space of organizational effectiveness has led to a sense of confusion and chaos in the literature, as well as to multiple models of the construct. What criteria are legitimate indicators of effectiveness (and therefore inside the construct space) are unknown as are the criteria that are not legitimate indicators of effectiveness (and therefore outside the construct space). For example, "member satisfaction" has been used as a *predictor* of effectiveness (outside the construct space), as an *indicator* of effectiveness (inside the construct space), and as a *result* of effectiveness (outside the construct space) (see Campbell, 1977; Cummings, 1977; Lawler, Hall, and Oldham, 1974; Miles and Randolph, 1980). Furthermore, different criteria have served as indicators of effectiveness even though they are unrelated or contradictory. Both efficiency (an absence of slack) and adaptability (an availability of slack) may be indicators of effectiveness, for example. Not only are they contradictory criteria, but, as in the case of member satisfaction, it is not clear what their relationships are to the construct space. They may be included in the construct space of effectiveness as criteria, predictors of effectiveness and therefore outside the construct space, or they may be produced by an organization's effectiveness.

There is, perhaps, a positive side to this lack of specificity of the construct space. Because organizations are complex and ambiguous, complexity and ambiguity in effectiveness models may be required to map the space properly. Such an approach would allow for a wide variety of organizations to be considered effective, even when they possess significantly different characteristics. It also allows criteria to be included which an organization's constituencies may not see as important but which could be critical to the survival of the organization in the future.

3. *The best criteria for assessing organizational effectiveness are unknown.* It follows that where the construct space of effectiveness is uncertain, its measurement will be equally uncertain. "One reason that the best criteria for assessing effectiveness are unknown is that organizational effectiveness is inherently subjective, and it is based on the personal values and preferences of individuals" (Cameron and Whetten, 1983, p. 11). However, several problems lead to an "obfuscation" of preferences as effectiveness criteria. First, individuals frequently cannot identify their own preferences for an organization, or their preferences change, sometimes dramatically, over time and with changing circumstances. Likewise, a variety of contradictory preferences are often pursued simultaneously in an organization (e.g., the contradiction implicit in a staff's insistence on solemn quiet in the library while library administration seeks to promote active student-student and student-librarian interaction in the pursuit of information). And, finally, the expressed preferences of strategic constituencies frequently are unrelated or negatively related to one another (e.g., students just want the information they need, while faculty want them to learn how to find that information on their own), and may very well be unrelated to the ultimate evaluation of the effectiveness of the organization as a whole.

If there cannot be one universal model of organizational effectiveness (because there is no universal theory of organizations) and there is a wide diversity in the use of the term "effectiveness" (that is, its meaning varies widely), how does one proceed? Cameron and Whetten suggest (and this is fundamental to the problem of criteria selection) that it is more worthwhile to develop frameworks for assessing effectiveness than to try to develop theories of effectiveness. While it may be true that the *best* criteria of effectiveness cannot be determined, it would seem to be possible to select *appropriate* criteria consistent with a particular viewpoint. As they maintain, the engineering of effectiveness is a more productive activity than is theorizing about effectiveness (1983, p. 267).

On the basis of these three reasons, Cameron and Whetten argue that in researching organizational effectiveness the only way to deal adequately with definitional and assessment problems is to make choices which limit the construct space so that the investigator can focus on a *limited* set of criteria. As with other complex constructs in the social sciences (e.g., intelligence, motivation, leadership) measurement generally seems to lead to an improved understanding. However, concentrating on measuring limited domains of the construct requires that the researcher make informed choices about the criteria to be included and the aspect of the organizational effectiveness construct space on which the research will be focused.

ORGANIZATIONAL CHARACTERISTICS OF ACADEMIC LIBRARIES

Because an organization's traits help the researcher define appropriate effectiveness criteria, it is important to consider the characteristics of academic libraries and some fundamental points concerning the measurement of their effectiveness.

Cameron lists four relevant characteristics of colleges and universities (1978b, p. 31). These institutions (1) are open systems in continuous interaction with several environments; (2) possess ordered and predictable relationships among members; (3) exhibit dynamic qualities in that organizational structures, boundaries, goals, and constituencies are changing; and (4) are loosely coupled systems (Weick, 1976).

Not surprisingly, libraries, as organizations within academic institutions, exhibit the same characteristics. Of these, the one most relevant to this discussion is the last. "Coupling" is the association the various parts of an organizational system have with each other and is usually considered in relationship to the tasks of the organization. Highly interrelated task systems where various units are very dependent on other units to get their work done (e.g., automobile assembly plants) are considered highly coupled.

Conversely, organizations which pursue a multiplicity of sometimes contradictory goals and where the units are much less dependent on each other for success (e.g., a university) are considered loosely coupled. It is theorized that coupling, as an organizational structural variable, contributes to the success of an organization by its presence in the degree required by any given organization.

In addition to being loosely coupled, libraries also appear to be "organized anarchies." Organized anarchies are organizations such as schools, colleges, large service organizations, business conglomerates, many governmental bureaus, research and development organizations, and formal political campaigns, whose parts are loosely tied together and whose subunits are largely autonomous. The major characteristics of organized anarchies, as described by Cameron (1980), are

- Goals are generally ill-defined, complex, changing, and contradictory. Organizational subunits are frequently pursuing goals that may be unrelated to the broader, more general organizational goals.
- Means-ends connections are not clear—that is, there is no obvious connection between the technology or the way the work is done and the outcome.
- More than one technology or strategy may produce the same outcome.
- There is little or no feedback from the output to the input, and little feed forward from inputs to outputs.
- Environmental concerns (issues of the outside world affecting the organization) differ widely throughout the organization.
- Widely differing criteria of success may be operating simultaneously in various parts of the organization. Pursuit of success in one part of the organization may even inhibit success in another part of the organization.

- There is often an ambiguous connection between the organizational structure and the activities of the organized anarchy. Rigid structures and hierarchies may be imposed on ill-defined processes.

While it would appear that libraries exhibit (to a greater or lesser degree) many of the characteristics of loosely coupled organized anarchies, most fit on a continuum of loose to tight coupling. Some libraries have relatively strong internal controls, coordination, and interactions, and their units may not be loosely coupled. With respect to an individual library, two examples of tight coupling can be noted: financial accountability and the presence of unionization. Unionization has sometimes replaced the older loosely coupled working agreements and relationships with formalized or rationalized agreements on salaries, working conditions, and the like.

Furthermore, there are instances of tight coupling which are typical of most libraries, tight coupling, that is, with other libraries. Cataloging standards, interlibrary loan codes, accounting practices, professional practices, and connections with the larger publishing and information-handling environment are some examples of coordinating mechanisms.

Nevertheless, as Orr (1973) suggests, the sequence between a library's resources, capability, demand, utilization, and beneficial effects, "should not be assumed to be more than loosely coupled, even when time lags between cause and effect are taken into account" (p. 319). He also suggests that an optimist would believe that the closeness of coupling will tend to increase as library management improves. But that may not necessarily be so. Libraries are required to pursue quite disparate and often contradictory objectives. For example, libraries are characterized by mixed organizational technologies. Technical services have the characteristics of continuous process manufacturing. Clerical public services have the characteristics of routinized service processes. Professional public services activities are highly nonroutinized service processes. Loose coupling may be a *sine qua non* of their effectiveness as it appears to be of academic institutions.

With respect to its host institution, it has been assumed that a library should be closely coupled to it. This is particularly evident in the matter of the library and library standards. For example, the "Standards for College Libraries, 1986: The Final Version approved by the ACRL Board of Directors" (1986) contains several standards (and comments) that clearly link a library's effectiveness with close association with the host institution.

Close association may indeed prove to be appropriate or desirable. However, it is unfortunate that unverified and untested assertions on the nature and degree of coupling between library and college have become enshrined in standards. Unfortunate, because there is evidence from organizational behavior research that would urge caution into such assertions. Unfortunate, also, because for librarians, demonstrating the achievement of standards frequently substitutes for demonstrating true effectiveness.

DeProspo and Altman (1972) and Baker and Lancaster (1991) offer very insightful criticism into the inadequacy of standards as substitutes for effectiveness measures. The former note that in the absence of workable ways of evaluating the effectiveness of libraries, the profession has adopted standards as a way to measure accomplishments, because standards are easy to apply and (in 1972) were thought to be effective in securing additional money from funding agencies. DeProspo and Altman further note that in accepting standards, librarians imply that "descriptive statistics collected by libraries are meaningful indices of performance and that quality is inextricably bound to quantity" (1972, p. 23). Both, the authors contend, are highly questionable assumptions.

Baker and Lancaster observe that library standards tend to be guidelines rather than the true enforceable standards one encounters in manufacturing and engineering. Standards emphasize inputs rather than outputs (services) and are based on current practices in institutions generally accepted to be "good." Because of the considerable diversity among libraries it is difficult and probably dangerous to attempt to develop precise quantifiable standards. In general, then, according to these authors, standards may have some value as procedural guidelines, but are too broad and imprecise to be used as detailed criteria.

The relationship of library standards, effectiveness, and colleges and universities was also explored in a major 1980 conference on that topic (Virgo and Yuro, 1981). The six regional accreditation associations at the conference gave clear expression to their traditional view that libraries must be evaluated in the context of the institution's overall evaluation. In so doing, they implicitly assume that libraries and learning are tightly coupled. Again, they may be. But the absence of empirical evidence defining this relationship leaves us with no way to demonstrate how either the library or the host contributes to the other's effectiveness.

The regional accrediting associations typically justify their position by broad reference to the presumed connections between the library, its materials, services, and staff, and learning. For example, the current standards of the Middle States Association of Colleges and Schools (Middle States Association of Colleges and Schools, 1988) begin with the assumption that a good library is related to real learning, stating:

> The centrality of a library/learning resources center in the educational mission of an institution deserves more than rhetoric and must be supported by more than lip service. An active and continuous program of bibliographic instruction is essential to realize this goal. . . . The quality of the holdings, their relevance to the institution's current educational programs, and the frequency of their use are essential characteristics of an effective center. Faculty should

> demonstrate the importance of books and other materials in their teaching, research, and in their own personal growth and development. . . . Librarians and other resources center staff must demonstrate their professional competence on the basis of criteria comparable to those for other faculty and staff. (pp. 35–36)

Though few of us would challenge the assumption that books and learning are related (it seems intuitively obvious that "real" learning involves "real" scholarship and that implies a "real" and effective interaction with books and journals), it is hard not to ask some very direct, very tough questions about what this relationship is, how it is operationalized, and how it is measured or evaluated. Where is the empirical evidence that says that a "good" library is essential to "good" learning? Where is the research that demonstrates how a library can—or how an "effective" library does—contribute to learning? And where are the tools librarians need to evaluate the real impact (or lack of impact) of their efforts?

It may be that libraries are only loosely coupled to learning. This could explain the absence of empirical evidence for tight coupling. It may even be that the relationship which we should be examining is that between learning and information, not learning and libraries. A library is, after all, only one element of the total information environment on a college campus, an environment which also includes textbooks, lecture notes, instructional media, computers, and even the personal information the student inevitably brings to any learning experience. Perhaps accrediting agencies would be better advised to ask how effectively an institution's curricula and pedagogies bring about meaningful engagement between the student and information (defined broadly) than to ask questions about the centrality of the library to its educational mission.

In any case, the unverified assumption that libraries are, or should be, tightly coupled to their host institutions has had a number of unfortunate results. DeProspo and Altman's comments seem painfully applicable here: how often do librarians (and college and university administrators) substitute descriptive library statistics for real evidence that an institution's library contributes to its host's overall effectiveness? It is interesting in this regard that of the fifteen or so evaluation measures proposed in the recently published *Measuring Academic Library Performance: A Practical Approach* (Van House, Weil, and McClure, 1990), not one of them attempts to measure whether (much less, in what ways) the library was at all relevant to student learning. Perhaps even more discouraging than that, the Middle States standards themselves seem to encourage institutions to focus on library output measures (as opposed to real "outcomes" measures), implying, as they do, that being able to demonstrate an active bibliographic instruction program, a quality collection, high circulation rates, and librarians whose credentials compare favorably with those of teaching faculty are all that is required to demonstrate the significance of the library to the intellectual life of the institution.

This discussion of loose versus tight coupling, both within the library and between the library and its environment, is important because it helps to point out why a multiplicity of criteria may be needed. If libraries were known to be exclusively tightly coupled, a narrow set of effectiveness criteria could probably be defined. However, since they can be both tightly and loosely coupled, a broad and comprehensive set of criteria would seem to be required.

EFFECTIVENESS CRITERIA IN THE LIBRARY LITERATURE

Very little theoretical justification is presented in the literature for most criteria proposed for assessing organizational effectiveness. Furthermore, there is a persistence of confusion in the definition and use of expressions such as "criterion," "standard," "performance measure," "measurement," "evaluation," "efficiency," and "effectiveness." To confuse matters even further, writers, in an effort to clarify matters, will sometimes complicate them instead by introducing combinations of terms, which create new definitional problems. For example, Evans, Borko, and Ferguson (1972) use the expressions "criterion concepts" and "criterion measures." Criterion concepts are criteria grouped according to the aspect of the library system being evaluated. They recognize five such criterion concepts: accessibility, cost, user satisfaction, response time, cost/benefit ratio, and use. Examples of criterion measures are (using the "cost" concept): staff size, staff skill and characteristics, unit cost, ratio of book budget to users.

Implicit in the list of Evans et al. is the inclusion of "benefits" in their definition of library effectiveness. But as Orr (1973) has suggested, "effectiveness" is really only the measurement of how "good" library service is. The issue of benefits, or how much good the service does, is probably beyond the reach of effectiveness measurement, using techniques now available.

Wessel, Cohrssen, and Moore (1968) attempt to cut through the semantic thicket and define "criterion" as "a requirement on which a judgment or decision may be based." They then define a "standard" as "something set up or established by authority as a rule for the measure of quantity, extent, value, or quality." At the third level, they define "effectiveness" as "the extent or degree to which a particular thing fulfills the mission, goal, or objective for which it was performed, that is, the degree to which it meets the standard set by authority." Following that, they define "efficiency" as "effective operation as measured by comparing production with cost." They summarize their discussion by observing that it is not possible to establish specific levels such as efficiency without first establishing more

Table 5–1
Four Classes of Evaluation with Examples

I Inputs (Resources)	II Processes (Capability)	III Outputs (Utilization)	IV Impact (Benefits)
Budget Space Salaries Gifts	Methods Collections Security Catalog Cooperative arrangements Staff Training User Education policies Planning/Organizing	Use of Services	Impact on objectives of parent organization—learning, performance, etc. Cost savings compared to use of alternate sources of information or productivity Improved decisions Improved level of education Better use of leisure

(from Knightly, 1979, p.174)

generic levels such as effectiveness. In turn, measures of "effectiveness" cannot be established without first establishing "standards" and more generic than standards, "criteria."

Knightly (1979), in a neglected study entitled "Overcoming the Criterion Problem in the Evaluation of Library Performance," goes a long way toward offering a structure for examining library performance criteria, data on criteria in wide usage, and guidelines for library managers for selecting appropriate criteria for the evaluation of their organizations. In an analysis of sixty-two library annual reports (of which two-thirds were academic libraries), he recognizes that there are *types* (or sources) of measurement criteria and *classes* of evaluation. Table 5–1 lists his four classes of evaluation, with examples, and Table 5–2 describes the results of his analysis of the library annual reports, showing the classes of evaluation and the types of measurement criteria.

The foregoing discussion illustrates

- The confusion in the field regarding not only the definition of effectiveness but also the definitions of terms used to identify effectiveness;
- The inability of the researcher in library effectiveness to build on a network of developed theory and investigation;
- The requirement that the investigator pick a place from which to study,

Table 5–2
Evaluation Grid: Types of Measurement Criteria and Classes of Evaluation Used in Sixty-two Annual Reports

	Inputs/ Resources	Processes/ Capability	Outputs/ Utilization	Impact/ Benefits	Totals	
User opinion	0	0	9	0	9	1.1%
Expert opinion	6	145	8	0	159	20.3%
Standards/formulas	0	2	0	0	2	0.2%
Comparison to others	4	10	1	0	15	1.9%
Quantifiable measures	4	231	227	0	462	39.6%
Costs	106	5	0	0	111	14.3%
Other*	16	0	0	0	16	2.0%
Totals	136	393	245	0	74	99.6%
% of total samples	17.5%	50.7%	31.6%	0%	99.8%	

*other includes buildings, building additions

(from Knightly, 1979, p.175)

define terms, and by attempting to relate the new study to other research, begin creating a ''nomological'' network of effectiveness studies (yet another study unrelated to any other organizational effectiveness research would seem to serve no useful purpose); and

- The reality that although it is possible to derive hundreds of effectiveness criteria from the literature, it is very difficult to determine whether they were appropriately selected and employed.

Chapter 6

RESEARCH METHODOLOGY

In the following chapter, we describe the means we used to conduct a study of academic library effectiveness based on Cameron's principles of organizational effectiveness. As we have noted in the preceding chapters, Cameron's research in college and university effectiveness has demonstrated that this construct is both multivariate and multidimensional. That is, many elements of organizational behavior must be used in judging organizational effectiveness (multivariate), and the effectiveness of the organization is expressed in the simultaneous relative effectiveness of sets of organizational behaviors and attitudes (multidimensional). The question before us, then, is whether these principles hold for the effectiveness of academic libraries.

The research involved the following stages: (1) the identification and generation of a criteria list; (2) the development of a test instrument (a questionnaire) to be used to measure the elements of effectiveness implicit in the criteria list; (3) pretesting the criteria list and the questionnaire in order to refine the language and the emphases; (4) administering the questionnaire to academic libraries in several Middle Atlantic states; and (5) analyzing the collected data.

CRITERIA SELECTION

As we have noted earlier, because effectiveness is a construct and thus a subjective mental image, its extent or space cannot be determined precisely. It then follows that the best criteria for assessing it cannot be known. This presents the investigator with a serious dilemma. However, as we have also argued, while it may be true that the best criteria of effectiveness cannot be known, it should be possible to make good definitional and assessment choices so that the investigator can focus on a limited but appropriate set of criteria. In so doing we should not expect that we have measured the full extent of effectiveness, but in the act of measurement we can begin to contribute to an increased understanding of the range of the construct.

The criteria were generated from a review of the literature, from informal discussions with library directors and other library decision makers, and from personal experience. The objective was to establish a comprehensive list of criteria presumed to be indicators of library effectiveness. No attempt was made, however, to establish an exhaustive list of criteria.

There were eight major sources which either contained or implied a large number of relevant criteria: Buckland (1983), Bommer and Chorba (1982), Lynch and Eckard (1981), American Library Association (1980), Knightly (1979), Du Mont and Du Mont (1979), Lancaster (1977), Evans, Borko, and Ferguson (1972), and Wessel, Cohrssen, and Moore (1967–1969). The criteria chosen were those which appeared to relate to more than one aspect of library organization (input, process, output, environment). The inclusion of a set of environment-related criteria was considered important because academic libraries are open systems which must interact with their external context in order to accomplish their tasks.

The selection of criteria was directed by answers given to seven "decision guides" proposed by Cameron and Whetten (1983) as a way to begin to map the construct space of effectiveness. Cameron and Whetten argue that if these guides were widely used (e.g., used in every assessment of organizational effectiveness and in every project designed to improve organizational effectiveness), they would provide a general framework within which research could be compared and, in so doing, help in the development of a cumulative literature in the field.

The guides are based on three simple principles recognized and articulated by Cameron and Whetten. In summary, the principles state that the criteria selected must be broad enough and important enough to encompass the full complexity and richness of the organization to be studied, but should not be artifically extended to include criteria unrelated to the organization.

First, the construct cannot be so narrowly defined in an investigation as to make it useless in a practical sense. At its heart, effectiveness is an intensely practical matter. From the viewpoint of managers it is the complex and contradictory nature of organizational effectiveness that provides its utility. Because of its complexity it is inappropriate to rely on univariate measures of effectiveness. If a measuring device must be as complex as the phenomenon it is measuring, multiple indicators of effectiveness are essential. Complexity must be included in the assessment.

On the other hand, criteria to be included should match the organizational setting in which they are applied. No useful purpose is served in randomly selecting indicators of effectiveness just to make the assessment broader or to increase complexity.

But most critically, criteria must be central to the interests of some important constituency. Unlike many other constructs in the social sciences, effectiveness is based on the preferences and values of individuals.

This suggests that assessing effectiveness is at least partly a political effort and that criteria selection has organizational political consequences. This political aspect is an inevitable result of the subjective and highly interpersonal nature of effectiveness and should not be construed as a negative. Organizational behavior is, in fact, the behavior of people and, ultimately, organizational effectiveness reflects the behavior of people working together. It is important that librarians understand that effectiveness criteria are not sterile absolutes learned in library school, but rather emerge from the shared needs and preferences of members of the organization. It is critical that librarians be willing to involve themselves in the mechanisms by which these shared values and preferences are expressed and operationalized. It is also critical that they understand the profound consequences that their choice of criteria carries for the library's and, possibly, the institution's well-being.

GUIDES FOR THE SELECTION OF EFFECTIVENESS CRITERIA

Because a major objective of this research was to assess library effectiveness in such a way that the results can be compared with Cameron's study of college and university effectiveness, the decision was taken to follow Cameron and Whetten's seven guides (1983) in the selection of criteria. As will be seen below, the guides are highly interrelated, so that making appropriate choices about one will depend on the choices made about others. As Cameron and Whetten point out, although no one choice is inherently right for any individual guide, some choices are more appropriate than others when answers to each of the seven questions are considered in concert.

Guide 1: From Whose Perspective Is Effectiveness Being Judged?

In any effectiveness study, a single definition of effectiveness must be chosen, however legitimate other definitions might be. More critically, however, the assessment of effectiveness must be conducted from someone's viewpoint. Effectiveness implies benefits/values. Values are held by individuals. Therefore, effectiveness can only be meaningful in relation to somebody's values.

For this study, effectiveness was defined in the same way Cameron defined it for his research in higher education, as successful organizational transactions. Likewise, the perspective is that of the dominant coalition, the group of people who exercise the most influence over the organization. Two reasons are advanced for using the dominant coalition. First, the incumbents in key positions are those most likely to be allocating the library's resources, determining its policies, and responsible for achieving its objectives. Second, the dominant coalition is the major users of data relating to organizational effectiveness. As Campbell notes (1977), there is no sense in collecting criteria that people won't use, or in building indicators of organizational health that are going to be ignored. Likewise, new measures of performance will be largely irrelevant if no one trusts them. It is commonly understood that it is an organization's stakeholders who ultimately determine an organization's effectiveness. It would seem to follow, then, that the perceptions of the library's dominant coalition are the ones to be sought with respect to library effectiveness.

An academic library's dominant coalition was defined as the incumbents in positions described by the following generic titles: director; professional assistant to the director; associate director; assistant director; head, public services; head, technical services; head, cataloging; head, reference; head, library-use instruction; and head, branch or campus library. This is an arbitrary, albeit, we think, a well-considered definition. Of course, there could have been variations in this list. For example, substantial and consistent users (e.g., a major research professor) could have been included. And, of course, one might ask how the perceptions of the internal library dominant coalition might have differed from those of the university's dominant coalition? It is very likely that there would be significant differences in the perception of effectiveness between the two groups. Such a question is beyond the scope of the present study, but it is discussed in the final chapter.

Guide 2: On What Domain of Activity Is the Judgment Focused?

As noted earlier "organizational domains" refers to the constituencies served, the technologies involved, and the services or outputs generated. When analyzing organizational effectiveness, it is important to specify clearly the domains being assessed. Lack of clarity on such differences may lead to confusing or contradictory research results as well as to incorrect or incomplete judgments of effectiveness.

In a general way, the organizational domains of library activity assessed included users, professional and clerical staff, services offered, collections and collections control, the technical system, environment, management, and financial resources, in short, all identifiable domains of library activity.

Guide 3: What Level of Analysis Is Being Used?

The perspective taken for this study was an organizational one. Thus, criteria, wherever possible, refer to more than one unit or activity dimension of the library.

A question that could be raised about the design of the study is whether it is appropriate to use data aggregated from individual respondents to represent organizational characteristics. It is generally understood that using data measured at one level of an organization to make inferences about another level is inappropriate.

There are two forms of this: the "ecological fallacy" and the "individualistic fallacy." The former refers to the errors which can occur when inferences about individuals are based on data from the group to which the individuals belong. The "individualistic fallacy" refers to making wrong inferences about an organization from data obtained from individuals. For example, if individuals are asked to respond only to questions concerning their units (e.g., catalogers about cataloging, reference librarians about reference work), and if the data collected are aggregated across all library units to obtain a mean score representing the entire library, the individualistic fallacy would apply, and it would probably be incorrect to claim that the study has an organizational perspective.

The answer would seem to depend on the design of the survey instrument and the organizational perspective with which the dominant coalition in the study is asked to respond. The design of the questionnaire used in this study was such that all subjects answered all questions, relatively few of which were concerned with matters dealing with an individual respondent's area of task responsibility (e.g., the head of cataloging was not just asked about cataloging, nor was the head of reference just asked about the reference function). Rather, they were each asked to evaluate all aspects of library service.

Likewise, all respondents were asked to respond to all issues affecting the library as a single organizational unit, and, as members of the dominant coalition, could be expected to represent the entire library rather than just their particular work subunits. In other words, judgments of effectiveness were made at the organizational level. Accordingly, the "individualistic fallacy" does not seem to obtain, and it would be reasonable to view the study as having an organizational perspective.

The initial factor analysis of the data was performed with individual responses to identify any underlying dimensions of effectiveness. However, the data were subsequently aggregated to the level of the institution in order to conduct a cluster analysis to discover any library clusters exhibiting common effectiveness.

Guide 4: What Is the Purpose for Judging Effectiveness?

An understanding of the purposes of an evaluation determines appropriate constituencies, domains, and levels of analysis. A clear statement of purpose is necessary in judging effectiveness because conflicting purposes for an evaluation create conflicting end consequences for the evaluator as well as the unit being evaluated (different information will need to be collected, different sources will be utilized, etc.).

The purposes of this study were (1) to evaluate academic library effectiveness as part of building and testing library organizational and effectiveness theory and (2) to establish a basis for a future examination of the association of university organizational effectiveness and that of the library.

Guide 5: What Time Frame Is Being Employed?

Long-term effectiveness may be a different phenomenon from short-term effectiveness, and in some cases, the two may be incompatible. Some organizations, for example, may consciously set aside short-term effectiveness in order to gain long-term effectiveness. Failure to identify the relevant time frame can invalidate the assessment. Furthermore, because effects and outcomes may evolve over a long period (or quickly in the short term), they sometimes cannot be observed if an inappropriate time frame is used.

The time frame for this study was necessarily that of a single point in time—a snapshot. A longitudinal study was not attempted. The limitations of this are acknowledged. Libraries may have had a bad year or may be recovering from prolonged fiscal depression or may be having an extraordinarily good year. Effectiveness criteria also appear to shift over time as the organization ages or responds to powerful external stimuli. For example, at one point some libraries attempted to develop comprehensive collections. Few, if any, attempt to do so now. Similarly, a new academic chief officer may unilaterally change the strategic emphases of a library.

Guide 6: What Type of Data Is Being Used for Judgments of Effectiveness?

In any effectiveness study, the researcher must determine whether objective data (organizational records; "statistics") or subjective, perceptual data (interviews or questionnaire responses) will be used. Objective data can be quantified (an advantage), may be less biased than subjective evaluations, and may better reflect the official organization position. However, objective data are frequently gathered only on a limited set of effectiveness criteria. In addition (and this is a serious problem with library statistical data), "official" data often relate to criteria of effectiveness that do not naturally flow from the library's central purposes (e.g., the dearth of valid and reliable outcomes measures). Finally, data which may be relevant may not be based on common definitions and, thus, may not be comparable across institutions.

In studies which utilize subjective data, a wider range of effectiveness criteria can be evaluated from many more perspectives. Likewise, the use of subjective data allows "operative criteria" or "theories-in-use" to be assessed. As always, however, bias, misrepresentation, or ignorance among respondents can influence the data's reliability and validity.

For this study, subjective or perceptual data were used. In addition to helping to assure comparability with Cameron's university effectiveness study, subjective data were used to avoid the problems with objective data discussed above.

Possible problems with subjective data were addressed in a variety of ways, although it is recognized that these problems can never be eliminated entirely. Respondents were assured anonymity; there was no incentive to be dishonest. Also, in an attempt to encourage candor, respondents were promised a report on the effectiveness of their libraries.

Potential problems of the lack of information and limited perspective were avoided in part, perhaps, by seeking responses from the library's chief decision makers. Furthermore, a large sample may have helped to improve the reliability and validity of the data. Nonetheless, these problems inherent in any research on perceptions remained and are considered in the study's conclusions.

Guide 7: What Is the Referent Against Which Effectiveness Is Judged?

A variety of referents are possible. In a "comparative" judgment the performance of two different organizations is measured against the same set of standards. Another alternative—a "normative" judgment— is to select an ideal performance level and compare the organization's performance against that. A "goal-centered" judgment is also possible ("have we reached our stated goals?"), as is an "improvement" judgment ("have we improved over the past year?").

A fifth alternative, and the one used in this research is a "trait judgment." In this form of assessment, the evaluator identifies certain valued organizational characteristics (e.g., "the organization acquires a sufficient amount of needed resources"), and those making judgments indicate the degree to which those characteristics are present in the organization. The trait judgment approach avoids asking respondents to evaluate subjectively or to express personal opinions about the effectiveness of their organizations.

In this study, the criteria selected represented traits presumed to be desirable in an academic library. For example, the acquisition of materials to support the college's curricula was advanced as a desirable characteristic. The judgment of the dominant coalition reflected their perception of the extent and amount of this characteristic possessed by their libraries. That is, the respondents were asked to judge how descriptive this was of their institutions (on a scale from "very true" or "highly typical" to "very untrue" or "highly atypical"). No attempt was made to assess how well this was done or how well the activity actually supported the curricula.

The list of effectiveness criteria appears in Appendix 1. It is organized by the input, process, output, environment system model.

QUESTIONNAIRE DEVELOPMENT AND PRETEST

A list of questions in Likert-like form or scale was developed from the criteria generated. "Likert," named after the man who invented the method, refers to the way questions in a questionnaire are posed and the way the questionnaire is constructed. It is a scale. That is, it is a device to measure variation in an attitude. In a Likert scale the respondent is asked to indicate degree of agreement with a series of short statements on a given range of responses. A "Likert-like" instrument is one which asks questions in the same way a Likert questionnaire does, but not necessarily to measure attitudes.

The intent of the questionnaire in this study was to measure the trait indicators of effectiveness as perceived by the defined set of library decision makers. Each criterion in Appendix 1 is keyed to the question or questions used to assess the presence or extent of the effectiveness trait embedded in it. In a number of instances, more than one question was used to capture the full meaning of a particular criterion. All of the questions asked for the respondent's perception; no objective data were collected.

All libraries in the Tri-State College Library Cooperative (Delaware, New Jersey, Pennsylvania) in institutions not offering a doctorate were invited to participate in a pretest of the criteria and the preliminary questionnaire. Respondents were asked to complete the questionnaire and to comment on both the criteria and the form and substance of the questions. No attempt was made to analyze the collected data from the pretest. The objective of the pretest was merely to secure competent advice with respect to the relevance, range, and comprehensiveness of the criteria and the interpretability of the questionnaire.

After examining the written comments and discussing with some of the respondents the issues raised, some of the criteria were slightly reworded to improve their clarity. A full description of the pretest process and results can be found in McDonald (1987).

ADMINISTRATION OF FINAL QUESTIONNAIRE

The reformulated questionnaire was mailed to all academic libraries in institutions without doctoral programs in the states of Delaware, Maryland, New Jersey, New York, Ohio, and Pennsylvania and in the District of Columbia (N = 264). The cover letter and the questionnaire are in Appendix 2. A list of questionnaire items keyed to the effectiveness criteria is provided in Appendix 3.

One of the objectives of the research was to collect data on the perceptions of a defined set of library decision makers, also called the dominant coalition. As noted above, this dominant coalition included all library employees with the following generic titles: director, professional assistant to the director, associate director, assistant director, and the heads of public services, technical services, cataloging, reference, library-use instruction, and branch or campus library. Because it was not possible to identify accurately the names of all of the people in the set of potential respondents, a number of questionnaires were mailed to each director and he or she was asked to distribute them to all appropriate librarians and to return a postcard (which was included in the mailing to the director) with the respondents' names listed.

To assure anonymity, the respondents were asked to return their completed questionnaires directly to the researcher. Upon its return, each questionnaire, already coded for the institution, was also coded for the title of the respondent. Only those institutions in which one-half of the eligible respondents (as listed by the director on the postcard) returned completed questionnaires were included in the analysis. Questionnaires returned by respondents from institutions from which no postcard was received were not included in the study unless it could be verified independently that the number of returned questionnaires was equal to or greater than 50 percent of those eligible.

DESCRIPTION OF THE SAMPLE

Three hundred eighty-four usable questionnaires, representing 131 institutions, were returned, an average of three per institution. This represents 49.5 percent of the institutions approached. The characteristics of the sample are summarized in Table 6–1 and fully described in Appendix 7. The respondent sample shows variation across institutional affiliation, location, institutional enrollments, the size of collections in the libraries, and the number and character of the staffs in the libraries.

The institutional affiliations were approximately evenly divided between

Table 6–1
Selected Characteristics of Sample Colleges Compared with Characteristics of U.S. Colleges Not Offering Doctorates

	SAMPLE		NATIONAL	
SUPPORT	Private	Public	Private	Public
	68%	32%	55%	45%
STUDENT FTE ENROLLMENTS	Under 5,000	Over 5,000	Under 5,000	Over 5,000
	76.6%	22.9%	75%	21%
LIBRARY COLLECTIONS (in volumes)	100,000 to 249,000		100,000 to 249,000	
	43.5%		42%	
	Over 500,000		Over 500,000	
	9%		16%	

state-supported and privately supported colleges and universities. The mode of the affiliation of the respondents' institutions was "private/secular," representing 37.5 percent of all returns. Of the institutions responding, 68 percent were private and 32 percent were public. Nationally (*Fact Book on Higher Education, 1986–87*, 1987) 55 percent of colleges and universities are under private control and 45 percent are publicly controlled. The largest number of returns came from New York, followed by Pennsylvania, Ohio, and New Jersey.

The size of the enrollments varied considerably, although the distribution was skewed slightly to the smaller schools, reflecting the national distribution. Of the responding institutions, 76.6 percent had enrollments of under 5,000 students, compared to 75 percent of schools nationally; 22.9 percent of the institutions had an enrollment above 5,000, compared to 21 percent at the national level.

The size of the libraries' collections, likewise, showed variation, ranging from under 50,000 volumes to over 500,000 volumes. The mode is the category 150,000 to 199,999 volumes (17.6 percent). Seven percent (N = 9) of the libraries had collections of over 500,000 volumes. Nationally, for the same types of institutions (four year, not offering doctorate) 16 percent of libraries have collections over 500,000 volumes. However, nationally, the mode is the category of 100,000 to 249,000 volumes, representing 42 percent of these libraries. In the respondent sample, 43.5 percent of the libraries have collections in this range.

Finally, the sizes of the staffs tended to correspond to the variability in the other demographic measures. Approximately 38 percent of the responding libraries had a 1:1 ratio of professionals to nonprofessional/clerical staff. The range of the size of the staffs varied from one to over twenty. Although there were returns from libraries with only one librarian, returns were also received from libraries with many librarians, and the range does not appear to suggest a preponderance of staff size at either end of the scale. Of all the returns from the defined decision makers, approximately 31 percent were from directors, with heads of reference and public services accounting for 26 percent.

STATISTICAL ANALYSIS OF DATA

The data were analyzed in several stages, using SPSS/PC+ and SPSSX statistical computer programs. After an initial examination of the data for measures of dispersion (or variability) and central tendency, a correlation matrix was derived (as a measure of relation) and the results were subjected to factor and cluster analysis. The technical details on each procedure or each set of procedures are contained in Appendix 5. In the remainder of this chapter, we will discuss, in broad and general terms, why the procedures were employed and some of the problems encountered in interpreting the statistical results.

For the initial examination of the data, scores were not aggregated by institution. That is, the data consisted of the raw scores of each individual respondent: the numerical value of each respondent's answer to each question. The first step in the analysis involved the derivation of descriptive statistics including the variance, standard deviation, mean, and percent of missing responses. Appendix 2 contains the questionnaire with these statistics for each question.

The responses to the questions (referred to hereafter as variables) were examined for low variance or high missing response rate for possible exclusion from further analysis. One variable (q42) with a missing response rate of 21.9 percent was removed.

Why was question 42 avoided by so many of the respondents? The obvious answer is embedded in the language of q42, which asked about the quality of written job descriptions in the respondents' libraries. If there were no written job descriptions, the respondents were instructed to not answer the question. It would seem obvious to infer that 22 percent of those addressing the question worked in libraries which had no written job descriptions. Other explanations, or combinations of explanations, are also possible. However, regardless of the reasons so many failed to respond to q42, the decision was taken to be conservative and "cleaner" and exclude this question from further analysis.

In its simplest form, variance is merely the measure of the dispersion or spread of a set of scores. It describes to what extent the scores differ from one another. Without variance, there is nothing to study. With too much variance there is, likewise, nothing to study.

Consequently, if every respondent to q82 believed that in his or her library it was extremely important to encourage the development and use of a reserve collection, the variance, or the measure of the spread of scores, would be zero. Everyone would have written a 7 as his or her answer to q82, and question, or variable, q82 would convey no variance worth investigating. (It might be important to note that the variance at issue here is that which would or would not occur in answers to q82 across all respondents from all institutions. The amount of variance in the answers from one institution might have been, in many cases, much smaller, reflecting internal consensus on the degree to which that library exhibited the presence of that trait. At this point in the analysis, however, we were considering data aggregated across all institutions; scores from individual libraries were not at issue.)

Instead, q82 was found to have a variance of 1.854 and a standard deviation of 1.362. The standard deviation is the square root of the variance and expresses variance in the same units of measurement as the observations (i.e., 1 to 7 on the questionnaire).

There is no rule on what constitutes adequate variance. Generally speaking, there are two sources of variability in a set of scores. Statisticians refer to these sources as "systematic" variance and "error" variance. In this study, systematic variance (i.e., the kind of variance an investigator looks for in this type of research) would arise from the differences in all respondents' perceptions of the presence, in their particular libraries, of whatever it was each question was trying to measure. Error variance, on the other hand, is fluctuation due to chance. Error variance is random variance due to usually small and self-compensating fluctuations of measures (Kerlinger, 1973).

Error variance in this study could have been created by mistakes in transcribing scores from questionnaire to computer, by computer computational mistakes, by tired respondents marking scores randomly rather than carefully and thoughtfully, in short, by any means other than differences of perception among the respondents. (However, it is important to note that computer errors usually have a systematic effect. That is, computer-related errors tend to repeat themselves systematically and are not merely an odd mistake here and there.)

Three questions were found to have a variance of less than one. There is, of course, nothing magical about the amount one. In our judgment, however, we decided to examine every question with a variance of less than one as a way to make sure that the questionnaire, overall, had sufficient variability. The larger the number of questions showing a low variance (defined here as less than one) the greater the probability that there were not enough differences in the librarians' perceptions of effectiveness, and, hence, not enough useful data to make the study worth continuing.

The analysis of the questions with a variance of less than one revealed, however, only three questions out of ninety-five with such variance. Because there was *some* variability in the answers to these three questions, the decision was made to keep the questions for further analysis. Two of the questions (q55 and q57) survived subsequent analysis and emerged as possibly important determinants of effectiveness as perceived by the respondents. The third question (q50) was eventually eliminated when it was found not to aggregate with other variables and, thus, not to be associated with effectiveness, again, as perceived by the respondents.

In the second step of the analysis, a correlation matrix was generated from the remaining variables (all original variables except q42 and q50) and examined for multicolinearity. Multicolinearity refers to a relationship between two or more variables which are so highly correlated that it is very difficult to know which variable is properly assessing the phenomenon in question. For example, any number of reasons could be given by car buyers for purchasing their automobiles. But, if all the reasons for buying were found to have correlations of 1.0, we would know nothing we did not know before computing the correlations, namely, that these were the reasons for buying the car.

Likewise, if after we had correlated all the reasons for purchasing an automobile, we found that "style" and "color" had a correlation of .960, we would not know whether it was "style" or "color" which was to be associated with the "aesthetic" reason for buying the car. However, if we further found a .250 correlation between "cost" and "availability of financing" we could reasonably assume that both variables were associated with the "financial" reason for buying the car.

In this study, the objective of examining multicolinearity was to identify and remove variables which appeared to be referring to the same or similar aspects of effectiveness. For example, question 16 states "Furniture and equipment are sufficient to meet the library's task requirements." Question 17 asks the respondent to evaluate the degree to which "furniture and equipment are sufficient to meet the library *users'* requirements." Even though the word "users" was underlined in the question, the high correlation (.8805) suggested that the respondents had difficulty distinguishing between the library *users'* requirements and the library's *task* requirements. This may mean that respondents did not notice the difference in the wording. Alternatively, it may suggest that in the respondents' minds, the library's "task requirements" are synonymous with the library's "users' requirements," *or* that in the respondents' judgment, furniture and equipment were equally adequate.

Ten pairs of variables were found to be highly intercorrelated. Each instance was reviewed individually; the variable kept was, in each case, the one which we believed best reflected the intent of the criterion from which it was derived.

After the analysis for multicolinearity (which led to the removal of certain variables as described in Appendix 5), the remaining eighty-six variables were examined to see which, if any, could be grouped together and whether these groupings appeared to be related to unifying themes or dimensions of effectiveness. The procedure used for this was factor analysis.

The term "factor" is a construct used to refer to a common entity or influence present in different variables. Factor analysis is a highly complex way of examining the relationships among all possible sets of variables in a collection of data to uncover, if present, that common entity or influence or relationship.

In the present study, it would have been impossible to "get one's mind around" eighty-six variables and all of their possible relationships. However, if several sets of variables could be found in which the components of each set were related to one another in a way that "made sense," it would be reasonable to assume that these individual variables were component parts of a "bigger" and possibly more important variable.

The technical procedures employed in this factor analysis are described in Appendix 5. Various statistical tests associated with factor analysis helped to confirm the appropriateness and correctness of the various procedures employed, assuring the researcher that confidence could be placed in the results of this analysis.

The most important result of the factor analysis was the identification of twenty-one factors, or groupings of variables. These factors were separated into major and minor ones: major factors having three or more usable variables. The statistical reasons for distinguishing between major and minor factors are discussed in Appendix 5.

Further tests provided strong evidence that the variables within each factor were composed of items with high internal consistency. That is, the relationship among these variables is such that they very likely are all helping to measure the same larger variable. These tests also help to confirm that each set of variables was distinct from every other set of variables.

But what is the significance of these sets of related variables? Inasmuch as they emerged from the effectiveness survey data, they would seem to represent groupings of organizational attitudes, behaviors, and activities having to do with effectiveness. It is likely that each individual factor represents a set of effectiveness variables that relate to a common entity or are component parts of a broader reality.

The emergence of these factors (the observation that the effectiveness variables grouped together into larger-than-variable-sized entities) seems to provide an answer to the question of whether effectiveness in academic libraries is a "dimensionalized" phenomenon (i.e., a phenomenon composed of sets of effectiveness variables). It is true that we cannot claim to have identified the dimensions of effectiveness in an absolute sense. Any number of variations on the research design (e.g., a different set of criteria, a different respondent sample) probably would have produced factors (dimensions) that were somewhat different. But in the very appearance of meaningful dimensions, we have powerful suggestive evidence for the validity of this understanding of effectiveness and for the utility of this research approach to the construct. The question of the significance of these dimensions is explored in the final two chapters.

Finally, the thirteen major dimensions were subjected to factor analysis to find the smallest number of variables associated with library effectiveness. The results of this procedure revealed four factors, or "domains," which are discussed in the next chapter.

Scores for each of the institutions on each of the domains were created by calculating the mean score for the variables comprising the domain. These were used in an initial investigation into the question of whether institutions vary in effectiveness and whether institutions group together according to certain patterns of effectiveness.

The method used for this inquiry was cluster analysis. Clustering is generally defined as the grouping of similar objects using data from the objects, and is part of the process of looking for structure or patterns in data. However, the objectives of clustering are varied, and many techniques have been devised and used, depending on the aims of the researcher. Lorr (1983), in summarizing these techniques, lists five general purposes for cluster analysis, including the identification of natural clusters within a mixture of entities believed to represent several distinguishable populations; the construction of useful conceptual schemes for classifying entities; the generation of hypotheses within a body of data by discovering unsuspected clusters; the testing of hypothesized classes believed present within a group of cases; and the identification of homogeneous subgroups characterized by attribute patterns useful for prediction.

The purpose of cluster analysis in the research reported here was to attempt to uncover libraries which group together based on their scores in the various effectiveness dimensions. If only random variation were found across the thirteen dimensions, only a limited use could be made of the predictability of the effectiveness dimensions. Each individual library would require a unique predictive model. It seemed to the researcher that a more useful approach would be to identify common patterns of effectiveness on the thirteen dimensions (as represented by the domains) as the basis for subsequent research which would focus on trying to explain the significant differences in those dimensions.

There is a very large number of clustering techniques, and the investigator is forced to choose among a bewildering array of algorithms. Seber (1984, p. 347) discusses a classification of cluster methods based on forty-five characteristics and points out that the number of conceivable categories of methods is of the order 2 to the 45th (or more than 35 trillion choices).

Faced with this array, the decision was taken to use techniques which had become generally accepted in the social sciences, which were accessible through computer-based statistical programs, and which produced interpretable results (a significant goal in exploratory research). The two sources for the techniques adopted were Lorr (1983) and the documentation for SPSS PC+, specifically, Norusis (1986).

Chapter 7

RESULTS AND DISCUSSION

We now examine the results of our analysis: the dimensions and domains of effectiveness, the clustering of libraries according to their patterns of effectiveness, and possible problems with the design of the questionnaire. (Issues surrounding the validity of the measurement of the effectiveness construct are treated in Appendix 5.) The discussion of the dimensions/domains and the clusters in this chapter seeks to highlight issues of major interest; the implications of the research results as well as areas for further investigation are explored in more detail in Chapters 8 and 9.

DIMENSIONS OF EFFECTIVENESS

A major result of the investigation is the confirmation that academic library effectiveness, as perceived by the library dominant coalition, is composed of many dimensions and is not a univariate phenomenon. In this study, thirteen major dimensions and seven minor dimensions were identified. These are based on librarians' responses to the questionnaire, drawn from academic library effectiveness criteria. Appendix 6 contains a full list of the variables (questionnaire items) which compose each dimension.

The thirteen major dimensions are

Library Collection Adequacy: Criteria indicating sufficiency of support for user demands by the existing collection and additions to it, and the adequacy of the annual budget (Factor Three).

Bibliographic Access/Use of Library's Collections: Criteria indicating degree of faculty and student use of on-site collections and services and the cataloging system (Factor Four).

Bibliographic Access/Use of Extramural Library Collections: Criteria indicating extent of library and user involvement in off-site libraries and collections and the support the library provides its clientele for off-site use (Factor Five).

Library/User's Shared Goals: Criteria indicating library goals development and the degree of involvement of various constituencies in their preparation (Factor Six).

Staff Development: Criteria indicating the extent of library staff involvement in developing their work competencies (Factor Seven).

Staff Size and Diversity: Criteria indicating adequacy of library staff size and skills (Factor Eight).

Librarian/Faculty Relations: Criteria indicating the extent and character of librarian interaction with faculty and college or university (Factor Nine).

Evaluation of Library: Criteria indicating the extent and character of the evaluation of the library's collections and services (Factor Ten).

Cooperative Associations: Criteria indicating the importance to the library of maintaining cooperative relationships with other neighboring academic institutions (Factor Thirteen).

College Support for Library: Criteria indicating the level of faculty, student, and administrative support for the library and the college's perception of the library's contribution to student academic growth (Factor Fourteen).

Shared Organizational Direction: Criteria indicating the extent and character of the library's interaction with its constituencies in developing policies and performing tasks and the importance of innovation in performing tasks (Factor Sixteen).

Librarian Professional Service: Criteria indicating the quality and scope of professional service in the library (Factor Seventeen).

Collection's Physical Organization: Criteria indicating the accessibility and efficiency of the library's materials shelving and storage (Factor Nineteen).

The minor dimensions are

Staff Morale: Criteria indicating the degree of morale in the clerical and professional staff (Factor One).

Collection Development: Criteria indicating the character and quality of collection development activities (Factor Two).

Facilities: Criteria indicating the adequacy of the library's facilities and shelving (Factor Eleven).

Library Perception of College Needs: Criteria indicating the importance the library places on its responsiveness to the college's goals, objectives, and curricula (Factor Fifteen).

Management Techniques: Criteria indicating the extent of the library's use of formal organizational administration practices (Factor Eighteen).

Materials Control: Criteria indicating the library's success and accuracy in maintaining inventory control (Factor Twenty).

Faculty Involvement in Materials Selection: Criteria indicating the degree and importance of faculty participation in the selection of library materials (Factor Twenty-One).

DOMAINS OF EFFECTIVENESS

Because there were thirteen major dimensions, an attempt was made to determine if dimensions could be combined into meaningful groupings which could render the data more manageable and, possibly, identify the domains of library effectiveness. When the dimensions were factored, four such groups emerged: Major Resources; Services; Library/Stakeholder Interactions; and Access. Appendix 7 contains the list of the domains with their respective dimensions and the variables comprising the dimensions.

There are two reasons for proceeding with the thirteen major dimensions alone, rather than including the minor dimensions in our further analyses. First, as we discuss in detail in Appendix 5, we followed Thurstone's (1947) strong suggestion that in exploratory research, the investigator should continue statistical analysis only with factors containing three or more variables (major dimensions in our study). Second, interpretability of results is a major goal of exploratory research. When we attempted to derive the domains from the dimensions using all twenty-one factors, the results were completely uninterpretable. However, when the minor dimensions were excluded from the second-order factoring, four interpretable domains were identified.

Figure 7–1 summarizes the domains with their associated dimensions. Each domain has been titled to reflect what appears to be the major thrust of the set of dimensions comprising it. Dimensions within each domain are not represented proportionally; the loading of each dimension on the domain is given in Appendix 7.

The discussion which follows centers on the domains. The dimensions are included as they become appropriate.

Domain One, Major Resources, is composed of Dimensions Three, Eight, and Fourteen as shown in Table 7–1. The association of these three dimensions is intuitively both reasonable and expected. The label "Major Resources" is intended to capture the emphases in this domain which are the major resources in any library, collection and staff. It is important to

Figure 7–1
Domains with Associated Dimensions

Domain 1: Major Resources

Domain 2: Services

Domain 3: Library Stakeholder Interaction

Domain 4: Access

Table 7–1
Domain One: Major Resources

Dimension Three: Library Collection Adequacy
Dimension Eight: Staff Size and Diversity
Dimension Fourteen: College Support for Library

note that the variables which make up Dimension Fourteen (College Support for Library) have to do with the intangible issues of intellectual and philosophical support (q5, "faculty support for library programs and services is adequate"; q4, "college support for library innovation is adequate"; q58, "the college perceives the library as having a positive effect on student academic growth") and do not include any explicit financial variables. This suggests that librarians perceive their ability to acquire significant information and staff resources to be related to their academic credibility.

Interestingly enough, the question of the adequacy of the library's budget itself was significantly statistically associated with, that is, loaded on, Dimension Three (Library Collection Adequacy), not with either of the other two dimensions in the resources domain (Staff Size and Diversity or College Support for Library). Neither did it load with other budget questions, or on dimensions presumably equally dependent on the budget, for example, Dimension Eleven (Facilities). This is not necessarily a new observation. Previous research has suggested that budget adequacy and collection adequacy appear to be related (Osburn, 1979).

The relationship between the library's budget and collection adequacy may need to be examined at two quite different levels. At one level, the relationship is not surprising. In times of lean budgets, it is probably easier and more acceptable for college administrations to reduce allocations for additions to the collection than to reduce the size of library staffs. This result, then, tends to confirm the special sensitivity of acquisitions to the vagaries of the institution's annual appropriations for the library.

Similarly, when the cost of a library's overhead is attributed to the activities with which it is associated, the collection-related budget can be a significant portion of the total budget. For example, in the University of California library system, the operating budget is divided into three approximately equal parts: (1) library materials; (2) technical services; and (3) reader services. Because administrative and other overhead costs are attributed proportionately to these three cost centers, the collection-related budget (library materials plus technical services) is approximately two-thirds of the total budget. Unless the allocation of the budget is seriously skewed, in this instance perceived collection adequacy might be taken as an approximation of budget adequacy.

Table 7–2
Domain Two: Services

Dimension Five: Bibliographic Access/Use of Extramural Library Collections

Dimension Thirteen: Cooperative Associations

Dimension Seventeen: Librarian Professional Services

But at another level, the relationship may also raise questions about how librarians define effectiveness. The results suggest that when librarians think of budget adequacy (i.e., when they rate the budget as being more than adequate), they tend to think of that part of the budget allocated to the collection (i.e., they also rate the collection as more than adequate) rather than that part of the budget which is allocated to personnel resources. Budget adequacy loaded together with collection variables, not with variables having to do with staff size and diversity, even though most libraries probably spend more of their annual budget on staff than on acquisitions. The question is raised whether this reflects a necessary relationship, or simply the priorities of libraries and librarians. In the minds of librarians, an adequate collection gives better evidence for the adequacy of the budget than does an adequate staff.

This relationship may be simply a reflection of the discretion librarians are given over the acquisitions budget. They are more directly involved with these expenditures and more immediately affected by them. However, one could ask whether this may also reflect the way the librarians conceive of the library's core responsibility. Is it more important to build adequate collections or to teach students to access information? Presumably, if the latter were true, one would expect an association between budget adequacy and the very expensive staff resources required to bring student learning about.

It is important not to overinterpret these data. Certainly the relationship is suggestive, but it requires additional and closer investigation. It is also important to understand some of the pressures which may influence how librarians think of the collection and of effectiveness. As we will subsequently show, library users (in this case, faculty and students) tend to define effectiveness by their ability to obtain needed materials upon demand. These issues, including the responsibility of librarians to educate users, are discussed further in the next chapter.

Domain Two, Services, is composed of Dimension Five, Dimension Thirteen, and Dimension Seventeen as shown in Table 7–2. The thrust of this domain is that of the library and librarians delivering services directly to the user and providing access to information beyond the confines of the local library.

Significantly, the five clusters of libraries all scored higher on Domain Two than they did on Domain One, as will be shown below. The former is related to internal effort (reaching out, serving); the latter, having to do with numbers of books and staff, is a quantitative statement of the willingness of the college or university to support the library, which, typically, is seen as inadequate to adequate.

It is possible that the five clusters of libraries scored higher on Domain Two because this domain consists of activities which are more directly under the library's control, activities which are cheaper and more accessible than those in Domain One. In other words, if a library cannot have an adequate (i.e., expensive?) collection, it, perhaps, can demonstrate its success by promoting access to extramural resources through vigorous staff activity.

Nonetheless, the observation that Dimension Fourteen (College Support for Library) loads on Domain One (Major Resources) rather than Domain Two (Services) suggests that librarians perceive that their colleges understand the "goodness" of the library as related more to traditional library measures of strength (e.g., collection adequacy) than to the information-dissemination domain (Domain Two). This may indicate that the respondents view their colleges as conservative in their approach to library service. It may also suggest that the expectations of the library continue to be dominated by faculty and student concerns based on a very traditional view of what a library should be and do.

Very clearly, a tension exists here. The library's major constituencies associate its effectiveness with its ability to provide an adequate collection. Librarians, on the other hand, understand that they will probably never be able to provide a fully adequate collection, as defined by the users (that is, having all materials which users require available locally at all times). Accordingly, librarians see the necessity of providing access to information beyond the local setting and place an emphasis on providing services that will allow that access.

The foregoing illustrates the changing nature of effectiveness. Had this study been conducted thirty years ago, just before computer applications for libraries began to emerge, this dilemma might not have appeared. If a library did not have what a user wanted, the user travelled to another library to get it or had his "home" library obtain it for him through "interlibrary loan." Before the rise in online bibliographic searching, library service was probably related much more to helping the user make good use of the existing collections than to assuring him access to the world's "virtual" ("logical") library.

Since that time, however, there has been a rapid growth in technology and an increasing demand for information, brought on, in part, perhaps, by the way in which computer-based bibliographic databases have exposed its existence and availability. It is a commonplace, now, among librarians, whose daily task it is to provide information, that no library can expect to have more than a very small fraction of the world's information within its walls. It is not unexpected, then, that Domain Two, with its emphasis on the provision of information services and materials regardless of location, would emerge as a dominant theme among academic librarians. It is also not unexpected that the mere provision of materials on site and the staff to maintain a building would continue to dominate the concerns of college administrators and faculty who are, by and large, not significantly involved in the professional concerns of librarians.

It is likely that until librarians can successfully educate faculty and students about the need to depend increasingly on access to information rather than on local ownership, the tension will remain. (Or, the tension will remain until there is full-text electronic access to all needed materials off-campus.) But why haven't librarians been more successful in educating their users about the realities of the information era? Part of the answer may be that they are not completely convinced themselves that access rather than ownership is the preferred approach. As was noted above, in the minds of the librarians involved in this study, the question of budget adequacy was related to collection adequacy and is not related to staff adequacy or service adequacy.

Domain Three, Stakeholder Interaction, is comprised of a large set of variables, all related to direct constituent interests in the library, as shown in Table 7–3. The variables involved suggest that effectiveness in this domain revolves around the existence of a strong sense of collegiality, among the librarians and between librarians and faculty.

A matter of considerable interest in this domain is the very large issue of faculty status for academic librarians. Dimension Nine, Librarian/Faculty Relations, is described in Table 7–3.

A recent review of the literature on academic status for librarians suggests that, although almost 79 percent of academic librarians have some form of faculty status, librarians continue to struggle with issues relating to its full significance and full implementation. The survey reveals, furthermore, that recently librarians themselves have been questioning whether faculty status is the most appropriate vehicle for realizing their full acceptance into the academic community (Werrell and Sullivan, 1987).

The association of variables having to do with faculty status with those relating to the professional interaction between faculty and librarians and the involvement of librarians in the life of the college which occurs in Dimension Nine illustrates that in librarians' minds, these issues are powerfully joined. The critical questions, however, are whether faculty status is important for successful professional interaction and influence in the academic community (as many librarians would argue), and whether faculty status actually facilitates such interaction and influence. The results of this study cannot answer these questions. It is clear that the two are related—

Table 7–3
Domain Three: Stakeholder Interaction

Dimension Six: Library/User's Shared Goals

Dimension Seven: Staff Development

Dimension Nine: Librarian/Faculty Relations

Dimension Ten: Evaluation of Library

Dimension Sixteen: Shared Organizational Direction

—question 80, the library considers it important that librarians are members of faculty

—question 95, librarians in this library are members of college faculty

—question 33, librarians and teaching faculty interact as professional colleagues in the pursuit of the college's academic objectives

—question 63, librarians are actively involved in the total life of the college

again, in the minds of librarians—but it cannot be determined from the data which, if either, is causative.

As we have posed the questions, they might best be answered, not by librarians, but by teaching faculty. It might be useful, for example, to ask teaching faculty to what extent they are even aware of the issue of faculty status for librarians. If it were found that many faculty are not aware of the issue or don't know whether librarians at their institution have faculty status or not, one might wonder whether their interaction with librarians was driven by perceptions of status or rank, or based on their perceptions of the relative value of the contributions librarians make to the academic community.

In view of the fact that after thirty-five years of struggling with the issue (the ACRL first endorsed faculty status as a right in 1959), it remains unresolved, it might be argued that it is time to move the debate from concerns for status and recognition to the broader one of a joint commitment to the college's well-being. This position has been gaining advocates in recent years (Query, 1985; DePew, 1983; English, 1984).

The fourth domain, Access, is concerned with bibliographic access and the physical organization and use of the library's collections, as is shown in Table 7–4.

The relationship of the variables in this domain is not unexpected, but the research provides empirical evidence for a possible connection among

Table 7–4
Domain Four: Access

Dimension Four: Bibliographic Access/Use of Library's Collections
Dimension Nineteen: Collection's Physical Organization

adequate cataloging, the physical arrangement of materials, and levels of use. Commonsense judgment might suggest that these variables are related. But other hypotheses are possible. It is plausible to expect, for example, a correlation between professional service and use of the library's collections. However, the respondents in this sample perceived use of the collection to be more closely associated with its physical arrangement than with their direct, professional involvement with users.

It is worth observing in this context that question 81, on the importance of providing full MARC cataloging for library materials, did not appear in this domain. Furthermore, it did not load in any meaningful way on any factor. This suggests that for the respondent sample, complete cataloging records may not be as important to library success as other librarians might insist. However, with the development of more powerful online catalogs that can retrieve data from all MARC fields, this may change.

As a final observation on the domains, it is difficult to avoid the impression that the librarians' sense of themselves as professionals is more strongly linked to the external information environment than to their own institutions. Granted that Dimension Seventeen (Librarian Professional Service) could load onto only one domain, it may be instructive that it loaded onto a domain together with dimensions having to do with access to extramural collections and cooperative associations, and not onto any of the other domains (e.g., Domain Three, Stakeholder Interaction), each of which had to do with a set or sets of principally internal issues. This suggests that, in many institutions, librarians feel intellectually isolated, even from their own academic community, and find most of their professional identity in relationships with entities external to the campus. Breivik and Gee (1989) discuss this isolation in relation to the educational relevance of academic libraries and to the current educational reform movement.

MINOR FACTORS

It should be observed that many of the traditional univariate measures of library effectiveness appeared as minor factors in this research. Variables related to collection development, library facilities, staff morale, and materials control all emerge uncorrelated with each other and the major dimensions. An effort to force their association with the major dimensions resulted in a set of uninterpretable domains.

This may suggest the need to broaden the profession's investigations into library effectiveness. Traditional library measures of effectiveness often tend to be "proximal" rather than "distal," that is, close to the library's routine transactions and processes, and far from the library's real goals. That is, they are often closer to inputs than to outcomes. Proximal measures, in this sense, are attractive because, on the whole, they are more measurable, more quantifiable, and seem more objective. Unfortunately, they are also more trivial. And as the research shows, such sets of measures may define too little of the construct space to be meaningful if effectiveness is as complex as this study suggests.

Nevertheless, questions could be raised as to why some variables did not load on certain dimensions when it would not be unreasonable to posit such a relationship. For example, why did Collection Development not load with the variables on the Collection Adequacy dimension? Should it not be expected that adequate collections are associated with development efforts?

A possible answer to this illustrates an issue addressed in the next chapter, that is, the need for detailed, or fine-grained, analysis of each effectiveness dimension. It also suggests the need (discussed earlier) for considerable specificity in developing effectiveness criteria and the reason general models of effectiveness (i.e., models encompassing all libraries in all institutions of higher education) are likely not to be successful.

As Miller and Rockwood (1981) point out, collection development is, at best, an inexact science. Citing Michael Moran ("The Concept of Adequacy in University Libraries"), these authors argue that there really is no way to determine whether a collection is or is not adequate. Formulas which exist are largely arbitrary constructions rather than validated criteria. And, although this inexactness need not concern research university collection-development officers who have the comfort of aiming for total coverage in many fields, or perhaps even in every field, it is an issue for small college collection-development officers. The small academic library has neither the funds, nor the space, nor the staff to attempt total coverage. Unfortunately, it also has little in the way of theory to guide it in its attempts at informed selectivity.

Miller and Rockwood cite no evidence for their position, but this effectiveness research does offer some support for their argument. Collection adequacy in largely undergraduate institutions may not be related to collection development because collection development, in a formal or rationalized way, may not be attempted in very many of these libraries. Librarians might maintain, for example, that once allowances have been made for instructional necessities, faculty demands, and commonsense purchases, not enough of the book funds is left to make collection development worthwhile. On the other hand, it could be argued that collection development should *encompass* these three areas, that a college library collection should consist of exactly these materials, properly selected.

There may be two reasons why librarians have not been more proactive about collection development. First, many librarians may tend to think of collection development as an abstract, scholarly exercise aimed at building the "balanced" collection, rather than as a practical, concrete exercise aimed at targeting available materials to user needs. Second, for the most part, librarians have not had the tools required to guide selection in these areas. In the absence of validated collection development mechanisms, and without the resources to effect total coverage, formal collection development in small college libraries may seem to be an impossibility.

In a general model of academic library effectiveness, the absence of a relationship between collection development and collection adequacy might be lost. If collection development in the university (or research) library component of a general model were found to be associated with effectiveness, college librarians might conclude that formal collection development efforts (scaled down from university size, perhaps) were required for collection adequacy. Instead, an effectiveness model specifically developed for college libraries and supplemented by detailed (and perhaps local) analysis could show that other factors are better predictors of success in obtaining collection adequacy.

INSTITUTIONAL CLUSTERS

Another major result of this research is the discovery that libraries vary in their effectiveness across the dimensions (as summarized by the domains) and that libraries group together according to certain patterns of effectiveness. The cluster analysis described in Chapter 6 revealed five distinct groups of libraries (Figure 7–2).

Cluster 1 (N = 23) is clearly separated from the other four on all the domains and suggests a set of libraries which have succeeded in large measure in achieving successful organizational transactions. Cluster 2 (N = 18), on the other hand, shows a rather large lack of success in the Major Resources domain, but demonstrates significant attainment on Domain Two, the Services domain. Their performance as measured on this scale then falls on Domain Three, Stakeholder Interaction, and improves very modestly on Domain Four, Access.

The contrast between Cluster 1 and Cluster 2 may reflect two distinct types of libraries, those with sufficient resources to optimize both Domain One and Domain Two (major traditional resources versus professional services) and those with more limited resources. These latter libraries, aware of their inability to adequately serve their constituencies in the

Figure 7–2
Cluster Analysis of Libraries on the Four Effectiveness Domains

Average Linkage Method, Squared Euclidean Distance

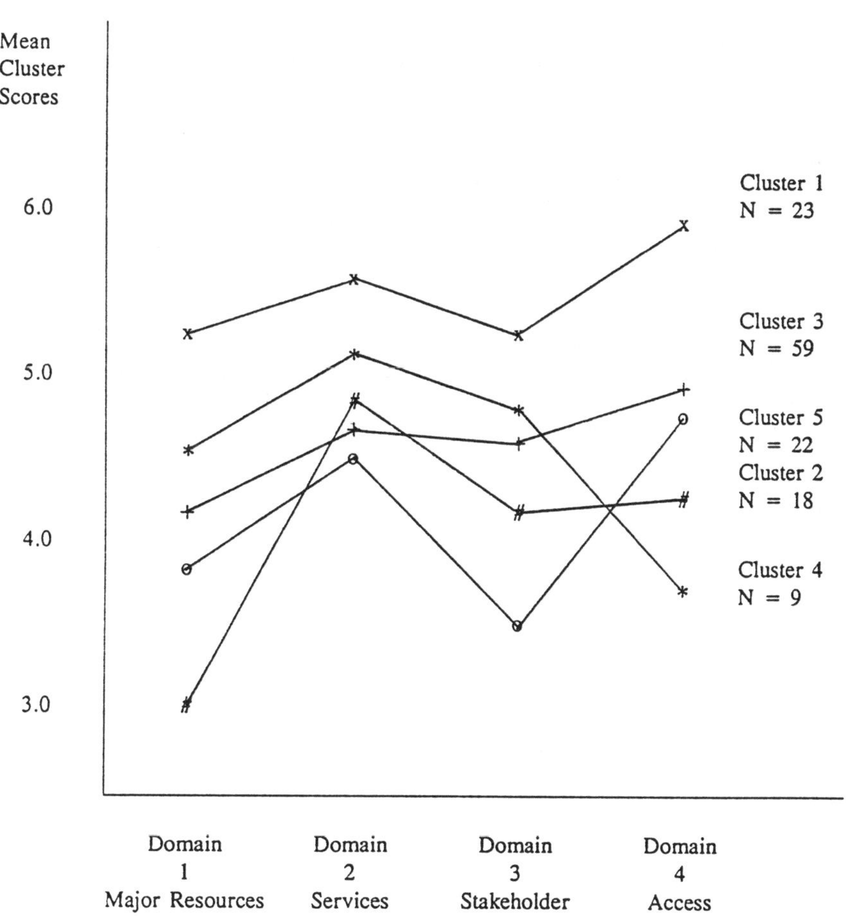

traditional way, may have chosen (or, perhaps, may have been forced by default) to emphasize the provision of professional service and to supply materials from cooperative associations.

Cluster 3 (N = 59), representing 45 percent of the sample, suggests libraries which, like those in Cluster 2, tend to optimize Domain Two, Services, but, unlike those in Cluster 2, are able to be more successful in Domain Three, Stakeholder Interaction, and Domain Four, Access. Not unexpectedly, a large proportion of the libraries cluster together here, to form what perhaps could be called the "mediocre middle."

In Cluster 4 (N = 9), libraries appear unable to provide the bibliographic and physical access facilities and capture the major resources needed to be perceived as effective.

Cluster 5 (N = 22) scores low on Domain Three, Stakeholder Interaction, but then recovers dramatically on Domain Four, Access, scoring very close to Cluster 3 in that domain. The precipitous drop in the score on Domain Three suggests institutions with relatively little concern for matters of direct interest to the people involved with them (users, staff, and perhaps, those providing the organization's resources, both on campus and beyond).

One general observation can be made with respect to these clusters which illustrates some of the differences that obtain when libraries are claimed to be effective based on a single factor (e.g., goal attainment) or a composite factor (e.g., the sum of the scores of subunit effectiveness) and when they are judged effective in their domains. After several attempts we were not able to settle on names or nicknames for the various clusters. This was unexpected. It should have been possible to find a term or a phrase to capture the mosaic of effectiveness in each cluster.

Subsequently, however, it became clear to us why we were experiencing such difficulty. Each cluster of libraries behaves in a unique and complex way across the domains and there probably is no word or phrase which captures the interrelatedness and nuances of each cluster's activity. To try to find such an expression would be analogous to trying to find a single or composite variable with which to describe the effectiveness of a library. Each cluster has attractive and, to a lesser or greater degree, unattractive aspects to it. Within each domain it might be possible to find nicknames for the clusters. Or, conceivably, it might be possible to name each cluster in relation to the contrast between its performance on two domains. But, if library effectiveness is truly multifaceted, it is probably not appropriate to attempt to summarize an individual cluster's performance with a brief and necessarily incomplete nickname.

HIGH EFFECTIVENESS CLUSTER

A surprising discovery in the cluster analysis is the apparent grouping of a set of libraries whose self-reported scores suggest excellence in all domains (Cluster 1). A comparison of some of the characteristics of these libraries with those of the rest of the sample reveals some differences which further research may show to be significant.

An analysis of the sample characteristics shows that approximately 48 percent of the colleges with libraries in the high effectiveness cluster have a private-secular affiliation. In contrast, this is true of only 37 percent of the entire sample. Furthermore, the mode of the enrollments in the high effectiveness institutions is the category 2,000–2,999. Whereas 13 percent of the colleges in the entire sample had enrollments in this range, 30 percent of the colleges with libraries with high effective profiles were in this enrollment category. Additionally, almost twice as many libraries in the high effectiveness cluster had collections over 500,000 volumes as compared to all the libraries in the study (13 percent versus 7 percent).

A discriminant analysis is required to identify the variables which distinguish the high effectiveness cluster from the rest of the sample. Nevertheless, from a review of the names of the host colleges, it would seem that highly effective libraries (as perceived by their dominant coalition) are those in institutions which are probably characterized as financially well supported, with a limited enrollment (admissions controlled by high entrance requirements), with specialized curricula (colleges offering degrees exclusively in highly specialized disciplines), and with a large ratio of books per student.

A complete analysis of the differences and similarities of the institutions within and between each cluster is beyond the scope of the present study, as interesting as such information would be. The amount of statistical data (descriptive, ratios, and "norms") available for colleges and universities in the United States is very large. For example, John Minter Associates (1991) publishes a handbook for classifying and comparing institutions which uses more than seventy management ratios (e.g., revenue contribution ratios, expenditure allocation ratios, degree completion ratios, etc.) to rank colleges and universities divided into thirteen different types of institutions. But the question is raised whether there is any theoretical or empirical basis for choosing among these ratios (or any other data) for comparison purposes.

Because both institutional and library effectiveness is a dimensionalized phenomenon, the problem of comparing and contrasting the institutions within and between each cluster of libraries is a complex one. Are there (statistically) significant differences between the host institutions of the libraries within each cluster or are they a homogeneous grouping of colleges and universities? Which data, if any, are likely to be meaningful with respect to differences or similarities in their effectiveness? What series of data should one use in examining institutions in each group? In our judgment, merely noting the differences or similarities among or between these colleges and universities, along a set of arbitrarily chosen variables, would not accomplish much, except, perhaps, give specious evidence in support of stereotypical ideas about colleges and universities and their libraries.

We believe that a study of the relationships between a library's effectiveness and that of its host institution will produce more light than an investigation of the differences among or between the colleges in the various clusters. Because effectiveness is institution-specific it seems counterproductive to compare institutions between or among the clusters.

SAMPLING AND QUESTIONNAIRE PROBLEMS

Two possible problems in the research design should be explored. These have to do with the sampling method used and the structure of the questionnaire.

First, although all libraries meeting the sampling characteristics were invited to participate, involvement was clearly voluntary. This means that the actual sample was, in some sense, self-selected. We recognize that less effective libraries may have been unwilling to respond and, thus, the data may be biased in favor of the more effective libraries. However, two observations can be made regarding this problem. One, the purpose of the research was not to determine how many libraries are effective and in what way. Instead, the objective was to try to identify the dimensions of effectiveness (that is, what effectiveness consists of), rather than the amount or range that might be present. Therefore, even if only the "most effective" libraries responded, it has still been shown what that effectiveness consists of and, having shown that, one of the major objectives of the study has been satisfied.

And, too, the study has shown substantial variability in the presence and extent of this phenomenon that has been called "effectiveness" within the respondent sample. This variability was self-reported, via the questionnaire, suggesting a general willingness to acknowledge success as well as lack of success in organizational transactions.

A second research issue that must be considered is the structure of the questionnaire. Deliberate design decisions were made with respect to the sequence of some of the questions covering similar subject matter. A question which might be asked is whether their sequencing influenced or brought about their loading into the same dimension. For example, questions 6, 7, 9, 10, 12, and 13 all relate to the existing collection or to the acquisition of materials for the collection. The intent in placing these questions together was to allow the respondent the opportunity to distinguish among the nuances of the questions. Question 6 asks if the existing collection contains materials of sufficient breadth and depth, whereas question 7 asks if the existing collection contains materials of sufficient currency. Likewise, questions 9 and 10 ask the respondent to distinguish between the acquisition of materials of sufficient *breadth* and *depth* versus the acquisition of materials of sufficient *currency*.

The high intercorrelations between these variables (as reported in Table A.5–1, Appendix 5) indicate that the librarians responded to questions about their collection's breadth and depth in the same way that they responded to questions about its currency. The research problem that is involved in this situation is the ability of respondents to give answers in cases of subtle differences. Similar responses may indicate that collections were similar in both traits. Alternatively, similar responses may suggest that librarians did not distinguish the two. However, if the questions involved had been separated, all that would have been known is that the respondents did not distinguish the two. Placing the questions in sequential order provides some assurance that the respondents considered the possibility that distinctions exist.

In cases of very high intercorrelations (above .8000), the decision was taken to determine intuitively which question better measured the criterion being assessed. The other question in the pair was eliminated from further consideration. In cases with intercorrelations below .8000, both variables were generally retained.

In some instances, the sequential placement of questions may have influenced their distribution during the factoring procedure. For example, questions 38 ("The library's collection development is well planned and carefully monitored") and 39 ("A strong effort is made in this library to develop its collections in response to changes in the curriculum and patterns of collection use") both relate to collection development. The decision to retain both questions was based on their moderately high intercorrelation (.7693) and the observation that question 39 related to a more specific aspect of collection development (responsiveness to the curriculum) than did question 38 (well planned and carefully monitored collection development). Because the questions were placed sequentially, the argument can be made that "careful" collection development (question 38) means to the respondents collection development focused on the curriculum (question 39).

As expected from their correlation, these questions loaded together on the same minor factor. This raises the question of where one or the other might have loaded if one had been eliminated or, similarly, how they might have loaded if they had been placed in different parts of the questionnaire. One approach to answering this issue would be to remove one of the questions from the factor analysis. However, the correlation was below .8000 which, according to Afifi and Clark (1984), is a very conservative measure. They argue for the removal of one variable only when the correlation is above .9500. Additionally, arbitrary deletion of variables can affect the identification of the factor model. Consequently, the decision was taken to leave both questions available for analysis. These principles guided the decision in all similar instances.

A further observation is that many of the strong dimensions which emerged contained questions from disparate parts of the questionnaire. This argues for the general reliability of the questionnaire. It can also be noted that this pattern of high intercorrelations between closely related questions was not consistent. Furthermore, adjacent and seemingly related questions sometimes loaded on different factors. For example, question 62 (relating to the librarians' understanding of and support for the mission and goals of the college) and question 63 (relating to the involvement of the librarians in the total life of the college community) might have been expected to load on the same factor. Instead, q62 appeared in Dimension Fifteen (Library Perception of College Needs), and q63 appeared in Dimension Nine (Librarian/Faculty Relations).

SIGNIFICANCE OF THE STUDY

The research reported in this book has addressed itself to three major questions:

1. Is it possible to establish criteria for assessing academic library organizational effectiveness and to develop an instrument that will measure library effectiveness?
2. Can dimensions of academic library organizational effectiveness be identified?
3. Can groups of academic libraries be identified which show high effectiveness in contrast to others which show low effectiveness?

An empirical and descriptive study was undertaken to ascertain meaningful and relevant criteria for the measurement of library organizational performance. Specific assumptions were avoided until the data gathered were analyzed inductively. The initial analysis revealed underlying groupings, or "factors," in the data, and further analysis demonstrated that the academic libraries in the sample grouped together according to their scores on these factors. The study has concluded that:

1. It is possible to establish criteria for organizational effectiveness of academic libraries;
2. It is possible to develop perceptual measures of library effectiveness and to organize them into a reliable and, possibly, valid test instrument;
3. Dimensions of academic library organizational effectiveness can be identified and thus, library effectiveness appears to be a multidimensional construct; and

4. Libraries tend to cluster together according to particular patterns of effectiveness with groups of libraries exhibiting high effectiveness in certain dimensions and low effectiveness in others.

The significance of the research reported in this book lies in the contribution it has made in three areas. First, it has adapted and applied a new approach to organizational effectiveness to academic libraries. Second, it has established the foundation for the development of an integrative model for the assessment of academic library effectiveness. And, third, it has begun to make possible the actual assessment of organizational-level academic library effectiveness.

The new approach to organizational effectiveness, developed and tested by Cameron, is rooted in his insight into the reasons for the confusion and lack of researchability of the effectiveness construct. He theorized that the fundamental problem was the necessary existence of multiple and changing models of effectiveness, not the competition between models for supremacy. He observed that insofar as there are multiple concepts of the organization, there would be multiple models of effectiveness of these organizations. He further observed that as the organization changed, the criteria for assessing effectiveness would probably change.

These insights led him to propose that any effectiveness research must flow from a clear statement of the model of effectiveness being used and the level of the organization being studied. Based on these principles, he designed and conducted an investigation into the effectiveness of colleges and universities. The results of that investigation showed effectiveness to be a multidimensional phenomenon, varying in its presence and strength within an institution.

Like the Cameron studies, the investigation of academic library effectiveness defined effectiveness in a way that captured the essence of many of the other models. It was also clear about the level of the organization being studied so that criteria were not derived from a less than organizational level and then used to make inferences about the organization. It attempted to use a comprehensive set of criteria rather than a limited set chosen for the researcher's convenience, recognized the inherently subjective nature of effectiveness and did not collect second-order subjective data (which is the essence of objective data). And, finally, it operationalized an integrative approach that had been proposed by earlier writers (e.g., Du Mont and Du Mont, 1979; Wessell, Cohrssen, and Moore, 1967–1969). By taking an integrationist approach, we are able to avoid arguing the merits of one or another model of library effectiveness, using instead a research design which encompassed the essence of each of the competing models.

This approach was subsequently shown to be applicable to other types of libraries. Childers and Van House (1989) used the Cameron principles in their study of the effectiveness of public libraries, showing public library effectiveness also to be a dimensionalized phenomenon.

A second important contribution of this investigation lies in the basis it has established for further research into academic library effectiveness. On the one hand, the research design itself has been shown to be a powerful and useful approach to the understanding of library effectiveness. On the other hand, the results of the study, while preliminary, have begun to establish a comprehensive model for academic library effectiveness that avoids the problems associated with univariate models.

In order to be considered complete, a model of academic library effectiveness would need to include a description of the phenomenon and a determination of the variables which distinguish among libraries of differing effectiveness. It appears that a preliminary description or a mapping of the library organizational effectiveness construct space has been accomplished here. What is now required is an analysis of the data to determine which variables maximally discriminate among the library effectiveness clusters and which variables account for the differences among libraries in the effectiveness dimensions. Once this is achieved, the predictive ability of the model can be tested.

It is possible that additional data may be needed for this further study. For example, institutional or "objective" data may be found to have considerable predictive power. However, as was noted in Chapter 5, perceptual data and objective data, presumed to be measuring the same aspect of a construct, may not, in fact, be doing so. Furthermore, as Cameron (1981) has noted, organizational effectiveness is inherently a subjective phenomenon. These observations argue that it may be necessary to acknowledge the critical importance of perceptual measures in the development of an effectiveness model and to reconsider the practice of using so-called objective data to validate the subjective evaluation of an organization's success.

Further research is also required to begin to establish both the validity of the construct on which the model would be based and the generalizability of the dimensions and domains discovered in this study. This research might involve (1) testing for effectiveness with the same questionnaire on samples in other parts of the country and (2) using groups other than the librarian (internal) dominant coalition to assess perceived effectiveness. However, using different groups—such as constituents external to the library—to assess the construct could produce quite different dimensions of effectiveness. Differing perceptions of effectiveness are entirely legitimate. Nevertheless, someone, somewhere, must eventually decide which set of perceptions is to be used in a given library, if it is found that librarian groups differ in their perceptions. Further research could examine those areas of common perceptions across groups, in an attempt to establish a "core" of effectiveness about which there would be little disagreement.

The formulation of an empirically defensible model for academic library organizational effectiveness might then establish a basis for studying and testing the relationship or relationships between a library's perceived effectiveness and that of its host, as measured by Cameron's methods. A question of continuing interest to librarians is whether and how libraries contribute to a college's overall effectiveness. Also of interest is the question of whether the college contributes to a library's effectiveness and to what degree they may be mutually interdependent. If both college and library were to establish a base of organizational effectiveness, a longitudinal study could reveal (1) the effect of the one organization on the other and (2) how and to what degree effectiveness changes for libraries and colleges, over time. Answers to all of these questions would contribute substantially to our knowledge of organizational success.

Examining the relationship between a library and its host is more than just an abstraction, a researcher's projection of what else could be done that might be interesting and fun. It may be more important than we realize. Earlier we noted the interest accrediting agencies have in the relationship between libraries and learning. Although we take it for granted that the library's effectiveness contributes to the college's effectiveness, this has never been demonstrated empirically. Perhaps because library effectiveness is so frequently defined in trivial ways, the connection between library and host effectiveness is not visible. We need to examine this relationship to understand it better, to define how one does contribute to the other. This understanding can then inform a fuller definition of library effectiveness.

Third, the research reported here has also established the context within which librarians can begin to assess their libraries' organizational effectiveness. It has also begun the process of making possible a "fine-grained analysis" of the dimensions of this effectiveness. As Cameron points out (1978b, p. 209), "Once an institutional effectiveness profile is identified . . . a fine-grained analysis of effectiveness can then really take place." For a particular institution, this could involve in-depth examinations of the variables comprising each of the thirteen individual dimensions of library organizational effectiveness. Alternatively, if certain of the effectiveness dimensions are not important to that institution, they could be ignored. In any case, such fine-grained analyses are not possible unless it is known what the institutional focus is. The conceptual choices an institution makes, in other words, are inherent in detailed studies of effectiveness.

For example, Dimension Three deals with the adequacy of the library's collection. A number of variables contribute to this dimension. Assuming the generalizability of this study, a library wishing to be successful in providing an adequate collection would concentrate (that is, do a fine-grained analysis) of the issues covered by the relevant variables, ignoring collection adequacy variables which did not load on this dimension.

A first concern, perhaps, if it were found to be a strong contributor, would be an analysis of q6 (the existing collection contains materials of sufficient breadth and depth to support the curricula). A second issue to study thoroughly might be that contained in q9 (the library acquires materials of sufficient breadth and depth to support the curricula).

But if the question, do we need to consider how to involve students in determining the adequacy of the collection, arose, the answer could be, no. This variable does not contribute to the library collection adequacy dimension, although a library might find in its analysis of q11 that, in fact, one way to assure that the collection is large enough to meet user needs is to involve students in determining appropriate size.

Although empirical research in library organizational effectiveness is not generally comparable with that reported here, existing research can be of significant help in conducting a detailed analysis of a particular dimension or subset of variables in a dimension. An example is suggested below.

In this regard, suborganizational studies, such as reported in Lancaster (1977, 1988), can be helpful. Although it would be inappropriate to combine these studies and call the results "organizational effectiveness," studies which deal with variables in various dimensions could be useful to a library in its fine-grained analysis.

For example, Dimension Five, Bibliographic Access/Use of Extramural Library Collections, and Dimension Thirteen, Cooperative Associations, suggest that sharing resources is an important indicator of effectiveness in the Services domain. Kent (1977) notes that while the actual effectiveness of resource sharing depends on the availability of appropriate communications, technology, and delivery systems, the associated problems tend to relate to behavior modification. Unfortunately, in most libraries, the full cost benefits of resource sharing are often not realized because it has to run in parallel with systems working toward self-sufficiency. But, as Kent further argues, as more integrated systems of resource sharing develop, it is likely that increased benefits can be gained from redistributed responsibilities and resources.

Kent's catalog of factors important in resource sharing could become the basis for a library to conduct a detailed investigation and program for improvement in the Services domain, confident that it was engaged in work which would improve its effectiveness; and that it was not engaged in work merely because it was fashionable or because the library thought it seemed a reasonable way to proceed.

Given the unique character of each library's effectiveness, each library will need to be assessed differently. Are there creative and broadly useful assessment tools which academic librarians can readily use to measure the success of their organizations? We examine one such possibility in the next chapter.

LIMITATIONS OF STUDY

As has been noted above, a very significant implication of this research is that which it carries for the development of a predictive model of academic library effectiveness. Further research and analysis is required to ascertain the relationship of the variables to effectiveness. The research reported here has discovered the variables and the dimensions which appear to identify the "terrain" of library effectiveness. Furthermore, it has discovered that libraries appear to vary in their effectiveness and group together according to patterns of effectiveness. In addition, one group clearly appears to be "better" than all the other groups. However, this research has not identified the discriminating variables among the clusters, nor has it determined the predictor variables in the dimensions or the clusters. It is possible that there will be relatively few variables with discriminating and predictive power. Accordingly, it seems inappropriate at this point in the development of the effectiveness model to attempt to evolve significant generalizations and inferences or to attempt to discuss details of the dimensions which further research may show to be weak or irrelevant in the model.

The implications and significance of this study are circumscribed by a set of limitations growing out of the nature of the study. First, the research data, not effectiveness theory, have directed the development of the effectiveness dimensions. This argues that there should be caution in interpreting the results. Although the institutional sample (131 libraries in colleges and universities in the eastern United States) and the respondent sample (384 dominant coalition members within these libraries) were large, it is recognized that the reported results may exist only in the sample.

Second, the perceptual nature of the data, likewise, urges caution in assessing the results. Chapter 6 discusses the precautions taken to try to assure accurate responses. Nevertheless, perceptual data present potential difficulties. The possibility of individual and library biases limits the assurance that these data accurately reflect reality. However, the analysis presented suggests some validity and reliability in the data. Furthermore, as has been discussed, objective data frequently are subjective data formalized and rationalized. And, more importantly, if organizational effectiveness is, at heart, rooted in subjective perceptions, perceptions are the "reality" with which the investigator must contend.

Third, the aggregated nature of the data may have influenced the nature of the relationships reported. Reducing the number of variables to a manageable level requires the researcher to rely on chance more than might be justified if this study were a confirmatory rather than an exploratory one. Without further research to confirm the findings, it is possible that some of the relationships reported are the result of statistical procedures rather than actual relationships.

Finally, the study has been limited by the static nature of the data. That is, no attempt was made to gather information on changes within the libraries over time. Rather, the data represent conditions as they existed in the libraries at the time of the survey (early fall, 1986). Unanswered are questions such as how did the libraries develop their effectiveness profiles and have their profiles changed over time. Only longitudinal studies can answer such questions. It is possible that over time effectiveness profiles may change in response to environmental influences, internal decisions to emphasize certain domains, and changes in the host college's strategic emphases.

Chapter 8

THE GRAIL OF LIBRARY GOODNESS

Although there is a consensus developing among researchers on the identification and investigation of organizational effectiveness, it continues to evade concise or definitive treatment. Coming to appreciate the complexity of the construct may encourage the investigator; such knowledge is of little cheer to practitioners who want to assure themselves and their constituents, with simple and direct empirical authority, that their library is an effective one.

EFFECTIVENESS AS AN ELUSIVE AND MOVING TARGET

Four aspects of the multifaceted character of organizational effectiveness in general, and of academic library effectiveness in specific, are considered below. These are based on the theoretical framework elaborated by Cameron and presented in Chapters 4 and 5 of this book. Each aspect has important consequences for the discussion of the contribution the present research has made to our understanding of academic library effectiveness.

First, it is generally recognized among effectiveness investigators that because there are multiple concepts of organizations, there are multiple models of effectiveness (Cameron, 1986). As our understanding of organizations grows and becomes more sophisticated, as new and different aspects of organizational phenomena are discovered and our insight into organizations enlarges and becomes more complex, our conceptualization of an effective organization changes, and no single model of effectiveness can ever capture the composite image of "organization," as it exists at the end of the twentieth century. Any attempt to measure effectiveness as defined in a specific model (e.g., the goal model or the system resource model) will capture only that part of the organization described by the model. Since aspects of the organization not included in the particular model will not contribute to the measurement, such an approach cannot lead to a full assessment of the effectiveness of the whole organization.

Granted that such may be true for organizations generally, does it necessarily hold true for academic libraries? Is not our concept of the academic library organization rather specific? And should that not enable us to agree on an appropriate model for the effective library? Do not Van House and associates (Van House, Weil, and McClure, 1990) capture the full meaning of academic library effectiveness by defining an effective library as one which achieves its goals (even as they acknowledge the difficulty libraries encounter in developing a unified, prioritized set of goals)? This last question is particularly important because the goal model of library effectiveness (in its focus on accomplishing services for a library's strategic constituencies) is the one employed in *Measuring Academic Library Performance: A Practical Approach*, a manual which carries the imprimatur of the Ad Hoc Committee on Performance Measures of the Association of College and Research Libraries.

Although it might appear that academic librarians are agreed (or are agreeing) on the underlying concept of a library organization, the confusion in the library effectiveness literature suggests otherwise. What model really informs the library organization? Is it to be likened to an academic teaching department in which librarians hold professorial rank, conduct research, publish, and govern themselves collegially? Or is it, perhaps, a professional bureaucracy or a machine bureaucracy (Mintzberg, 1979) with a well-defined hierarchy and rules promulgated by an institutional personnel department, more concerned with clerks and groundskeepers than professional anomalies such as librarians?

As the larger information and education environment in which libraries exist continues to fracture and change, the likelihood of librarians ever reaching consensus on what a library organization *is* or *should be* becomes remote. No single organizational model can be prescribed for the information agency which on one campus is a single traditional library unit, but which, on another, may be a "learning resources center" with extensive audiovisual responsibilities, or may contain various elements of academic or administrative computing or, perhaps, be a coordinating agency (with warehousing duties) for faculty and students who search bibliographic and full-text databases in homes, offices, dormitories, and laboratories.

It would seem, then, that if there are multiple concepts of library organizations, there will also be multiple concepts of the effectiveness of these organizations. Each concept of a library, based on its tasks and their organization, will give rise to a separate effectiveness model. But, for a library, as for any organization, measuring effectiveness as defined in a particular model will still be incomplete, failing to yield an evaluation of the effectiveness of the library as a whole. Likewise, in the profession at large, a lack of consensus on the concept of a library organization would seem to preclude universal prescriptions for the appropriate model on which to base the measurement and identification of effectiveness.

Second, it is generally recognized among organization theorists that as the environment changes, an organization must change and adapt if it is to survive. But an organization can also influence its environment, creating an endless loop in which changes in one create the need for changes in the other, which in turn places demands for changes in the first, again. This organization-environment interaction is basic to our understanding of organizations as open systems.

Likewise, as the organization changes (in response to environmental stimuli, because of growth or decline, etc.), it appears that the criteria for judging its effectiveness also change in predictable ways, leading to a new model for *that* organization's effectiveness at specific stages of its development (Cameron and Whetten, 1981; Quinn and Cameron, 1983; Cameron, Kim, and Whetten, 1987). If this is true, then libraries, as open systems, must find ways to match their criteria for effectiveness to their stage in a continuum of growth or decline.

But is the environment changing libraries? Are libraries changing the higher education environment? Is it possible that there is an interaction developing which will alter both libraries and colleges and universities?

Since 1945, libraries, but especially academic libraries, have been caught up in changes that are altering significantly the fundamental structure and integration of their work (*vide*, e.g., Breivik and Gee, 1989; Moran, 1984). Specifically, libraries are undergoing a paradigm change. In a lecture to the librarians and staff in the general libraries of the University of Texas, Austin, in the summer of 1989, Francis Miksa (1989) defined "paradigm" as it applies to libraries: "a paradigm is a pattern, especially a typical pattern, of behavior and relationships." Miksa goes on to point out that although Thomas Kuhn popularized the term "paradigm" by applying it to the way scientific discovery and advancement is accomplished, he was applying it to the way libraries operate and, especially, to the basic assumptions which librarians bring to their work and which shape their activities. It is at that level, he maintains, that libraries in general, but especially academic research libraries, are experiencing significant change.

Miksa argues that in the older paradigm (which continues to be a significant factor in most academic libraries), a collection is the beginning point of all considerations about the library and the work of its staff. Users tend to remain an undifferentiated anonymous mass. "When all is said and done, the business of the academic library is making sure its collections are built and available and giving guidance for their utilization to those who come to them." The importance of the collection and collection development in the older paradigm cannot be overstressed. Collections define the library, and the library, not the user, defines the collections.

After describing the older paradigm, Miksa noted how anomalies began to be introduced into the paradigm after World War II and with the introduction of the "information era." Librarians began to express a concern about the use of their collections. And as it became apparent that no single library could expect to own all the materials its users might want or need, regular access to the collections in other libraries was established and, to use Miksa's expression, "translocal" collections were developed.

However, the essential core of the change does not lie in what are usually considered to be the issues of the information age: an abundance of information, changing patterns in the use of information, large-scale adoption of computer-based technologies, and managing information with respect to its economic value. Rather, he asserts, the information revolution (in its effect on the formal control of information) centers on achieving specificity, on tailoring information and information services to the particular information requirements of users. That is, it has to do with, as he calls it, the widespread adoption of "a user-centered perspective."

Have not libraries and librarians, however, always had a user-centered perspective? Granted, there may be the anomalies: libraries with poor service hours; indifferent or poorly prepared professional staffs providing inaccurate information; poorly managed stack, interlibrary loan, and circulation services; and libraries with consistently and pathologically inadequate budgets which prevent them from ever truly focusing in nontrivial ways on the needs of their users. But we recognize these situations as aberrations. Professional practice, to the fullest extent possible, is rooted, is it not, in a determination to serve the user and to avoid the circumstances described above?

Care and concern for the user—certainly a distinguishing trait of competent and ethical professional practice—needs to be differentiated from the issue with which Miksa is dealing. His point is that technology, and especially information technology, increasingly is allowing information to be organized, managed, and disseminated in a way that allows the library to deal with user-centered issues directly, in their own right, and not simply as augmentations of a collection-based paradigm. Libraries, he maintains, are beginning to look at users' needs and information use patterns with absolutely no preliminary assumptions about the need to build balanced collections or to offer particular services. This means, in effect, to make the library's first concerns those which deal directly with the analysis and satisfaction of the users' information needs, whatever they may be and however they need to be met, and to discontinue building collections or elaborating services in the abstract. It may mean, for example, moving away from teaching library skills as an end in themselves ("one day you'll understand how important this is") to bibliographic instruction programs in which information-seeking skills are taught in an academically relevant, problem-based, curriculum-integrated manner. It may even mean finding ways to operationalize the growing understanding that the issue is information (wherever it is housed, needed, and used) and not collections, libraries, or library buildings.

However, beyond user-centered libraries, the information environment itself is creating pressures which promise to alter significantly the role of libraries. If increasingly faculty and students can sit in their offices and dorm rooms and homes and feel confident that they are getting the information they need by accessing online catalogs, bibliographic databases, electronic mail (e.g., Internet, which, of course is much more than e-mail), and services of various kinds (e.g., Prodigy), where does that leave the library? In one sense it probably leaves the library exactly where most people have always thought the library to be: in the place of providing information resources, mostly hard copy documents. But before technology made it possible to do otherwise, one needing information had to go to the library to use the various finding tools and be subject there to all that librarians might do—intellectually and physically—to make finding information and retrieving documents difficult or easy.

But as it is becoming less and less important to "go to the library" to use information-finding tools, the academic library is very much in danger of becoming a documents warehouse with, perhaps, a mostly print-based information finding side service for those unable to afford the technology to access information otherwise. Furthermore, if, or when, costs become reasonable, what is to prevent other information agencies from supplying needed documents, as is already being done in numerous instances?

What this suggests is that "librarianship" and "library science," *as presently constituted*, may be nearing the end of their usefulness in academic institutions. It may be, if Miksa is correct, that such expressions and what they denote are increasingly as useless in dealing with the *real* issues of information acquisition, management, and use as "hospitalship" is in capturing the real issues involved in maintaining or restoring one's health. As librarians consider the impact of these external changes on their activities, one would hope that their perceptions of what constitutes (or what should constitute) "academic library effectiveness" would change.

If the external environment is influencing academic libraries, are libraries also changing the higher education environment? This question is probably not difficult to answer. Whatever may be their potential as they change, and after they change, there is no empirical evidence that we know of to suggest that libraries, generally, are affecting this environment. Information technology would seem to be having some impact on higher education. But that impact is neither being directed nor shaped by academic libraries or academic librarians, generally.

Individual libraries may have an effect in their local environments. The library in Earlham College clearly has had a profound and continuing effect on the teaching and learning environment in that institution. And we suspect that college libraries which historically have received and continue to receive financial support seemingly out of proportion to their enrollments (e.g., Occidental, Trinity, Grinnell, Bates, Bowdoin, Colby, Mount Holyoke, Wellesley, Williams, Carleton, Hamilton, Vassar, Oberlin, and Middlebury) probably do affect their immediate organizational environment. It is difficult to imagine that these colleges would have the reputations they do if they had the resource-constrained libraries with which most liberal arts colleges must contend. On the other hand, of course, we could argue that because these institutions have a continuing commitment to the reality of excellence in higher education, it follows that they will have and support excellent libraries.

But could libraries and librarians, generally, have a significant effect on higher education? If they could, in what way or ways might this occur? Assuming that there is no value in effect for effect's sake, is there anything left on campus that is intellectually, academically, or pedagogically worth doing, which librarians and their organizations might take on, even if it required considerable change in them?

We think there is. Miksa has hinted at it but we need to make it concrete. The biggest single academic need on most campuses today is suggested by the expression information literacy, even though that does not quite capture the extent of the need. The problem, simply stated, is how do we make information seeking, information management, information use, and the associated skills, an integral part of the education our students receive? We will come back to this problem below, but in the context of effects on the educational environment of our colleges and universities, what other significant problem should librarians address? Or, put another way, if we do not do it, others will (e.g., our friends the information technologists already are having a go at it) and will probably do it rather badly, to the real hurt of our students and instructors.

If Miksa is correct that libraries are experiencing fundamental change, then it would seem highly likely that multiple models of effectiveness are needed for academic libraries. Change demands movement in the criteria according to which effectiveness is evaluated, not only generally within the profession, but also in highly specific ways for individual libraries, which are changing at different rates and in response to differing environmental stresses. It would seem reasonable to say that effectiveness is, perhaps, several moving targets, some overlapping others and some moving at different speeds than others.

But there is a third aspect to the elusiveness of effectiveness, revealed in its multidimensionality. The environment does not impact on a unidimensional library organization, nor is there a single external environment affecting the library. It would be more accurate to think of one or more environments influencing one or more of the dimensions at varying levels of strength, creating very complex stresses on the organization. Two examples can illustrate this.

Since the 1960s, libraries have experienced increasing difficulties in providing both access to information and the delivery of hard copy documents at a reasonable cost. Both are expected by the libraries' stakeholders. Access to information is increasingly governed by the producers and vendors of machine-readable data. Hard copy provision is largely in the hands of publishers and, if not available on site, it is governed by networks of libraries organized to lend or sell hard copy among themselves. Libraries, presumably, would like to be effective in both areas, and in the study some are. But if merely muddling through (not necessarily all bad, Lindblom, 1959) is not acceptable, success in each dimension will be at the mercy of two, possibly three, distinct and competing environments.

With respect to library employees, libraries (or library administrations) must, likewise, frequently deal with two or three competing environments: the internal one which requires skillful and balanced personnel management, an immediate external one (e.g., the institution's senior officers) which requires high productivity coupled with the parsimonious use of human resources, and the larger external employment environment, represented by the college's personnel policies and procedures and employment law which increasingly holds that jobs are property rights and due process is required to deprive anyone of a property right. How these environments interact and impact on the library is likely to be different for a large number of them, if not unique for each.

All of this argues strongly for the need for several models of library effectiveness which can be applied by various different libraries at various different times in their evolving internalization of the new paradigm. Alternatively, it may argue that what is needed is not *several* but *individual* models which might resemble each other but are, on theoretical grounds, unlikely to be the same in any pair of libraries.

Finally, it is generally recognized that a system cannot optimize all its goals and objectives. Either the system operates at less than optimal levels overall, or it optimizes certain aspects and is satisfied with lesser performance in others. Likewise, it appears that no library can be uniformly effective across all the domains. Librarians may choose or have chosen for them the dimensions or domains in which their organizations will be effective. The choices, moreover, may be conscious or even unconscious, as in library managements which simply let their organizations "exist," without any thought to actively shaping their character or purposes (Euster, 1986).

But the choices can also be conscious and superficial. The choices can be poorly informed, based on library tradition or lore taught in library schools, practiced, perhaps, in large university libraries, and passed down to smaller libraries without any empirical verification that these practices are good ones. These choices may not be thought through and consciously matched to the particular institution's mission and student needs. In other words, they may not be educationally responsible choices.

The idea of conscious choice, however, carries with it some inherent difficulties. And perhaps this is why so many librarians may not attempt it. First, librarians may disagree among themselves. The dominant coalition may not, in fact, be a coalition, but a very loose federation of librarians who have only in common the need to make decisions for the good of the library. Disagreement about what that "good" is can force decisions down to the level of a disagreeable but consensual mediocrity. Second, librarians may have a different perception of effectiveness than faculty or students. And, third, even if faculty and librarians and students agree, the institution's administration may disagree.

In most colleges and universities the likely assent and consent of its senior officers is usually a significant issue in decisions taken by subordinates. But most administrations will not be indifferent to the expressed desires and interests of their constituencies. Perhaps a key issue in having the administration agree to and support a particular definition of effectiveness is the presence of a *real* faculty/librarian coalition or partnership. How much, for example, has the failure of libraries to be perceived as educationally relevant led to their "problems" with the "administration," particularly, funding problems.

The chief financial officer of a small but vigorous liberal arts college on the East Coast once told us directly that he could not approve a much larger budget for his library's acquisitions because librarians were unable to demonstrate that the books on the shelves (and other information media) had any real relationship with learning. That they did was one of the unverified myths of higher education, and he would not pay for more materials until he could see a real and necessary link between them and courses and learning needs. The design of a syllabus-based mechanism for measuring the adequacy of that same small college's library collection (McDonald and Micikas, 1990) was, to his mind, one of the most encouraging developments in the whole issue of the justification for library allocations. The fact that the process was devised, tested, and supported by a library/faculty coalition made its impact on senior administration all the greater. The often-heard argument that if libraries were better funded they could be more educationally relevant, may be true, but it is not an especially powerful argument and has not seemed to be particularly successful in gaining additional resources.

Nevertheless, consciously or unconsciously, choices about effectiveness will be made. We need to understand that we must choose how and where (i.e., in which domains) we will be effective and then take leadership in actually helping our communities make those choices. We need to define, articulate, and consciously choose a model of effectiveness that has strong faculty support, one that is expressed in faculty/learning terms, one that is forged from a real faculty/librarian partnership. In other words, we need to recognize that making effectiveness is what matters and that making effectiveness is, at heart, a political undertaking.

As we have pointed out, it is possible that maximizing effectiveness in one domain (or dimension) could militate against effectiveness in another domain (or dimension). With many and possibly contradictory measures of effectiveness, academic communities may be forced to decide in which set of dimensions their libraries will be effective.

But it also appears that the matter may be more complex than merely deciding which elements to optimize. Effectiveness involves paradoxes, and these paradoxes or contradictions and internal inconsistencies may be essential for an organization's effectiveness. Cameron (1986) argues that paradoxical attributes give rise to creative tensions and that these tensions help foster organizational effectiveness. It is not just the presence of mutually exclusive opposites that leads to effectiveness, then, but the "creative leaps, the flexibility, and the unity" made possible by them.

Are "creative leaps" and "flexibility" and "creative tension" descriptive of life in academic libraries? Most librarians would respond with a resounding no. Furthermore, there probably would be considerable consensus among them over a hypothesis arguing that most college and university administrations (and, perhaps, not a few faculties) would be dismayed at libraries exhibiting creative leaps, tension, and flexibility. Predictability and consistency and order may be more valuable in a library than the "messiness" of creativity. One wonders, also, whether many librarians would like to be evaluated and held accountable in a truly creative environment.

For example, are librarians ready to make the leap from a focus on "faculty status" to a full working partnership with faculty, with or without faculty status? Likewise, are librarians ready to lead the way in considering a new definition of "librarianship" based on the large technological changes in recent decades? Are they prepared to move away from a warehousing mentality to a proactive, creative and critical, educationally relevant presence on campus where it counts: the classroom, the laboratory, the faculty member's office? This may be critical to the survival of the academic library. Why must we suppose that campus authorities will continue to assign 2 to 7 percent of their operating budgets to an academic service which, so far, has largely failed to demonstrate that it has any significant effect on the heart of the institution, its teaching and learning environment?

The principle of paradox that Cameron is proposing (1986) suggests that disconfirmation, contradiction, and nonlinearity are inherent in all organizations. This is a direct contradiction of most current models and theories of organizations, which assume consistency and symmetry. On the other hand, as he also points out, paradoxes are predictable and symmetrical by themselves. "They are both confusing and understandable, common and surprising . . . " (1986, p. 549). As he notes in his study of the effectiveness of colleges and universities, highly effective institutions tended to be paradoxical, performing in contradictory ways to satisfy contradictory expectations.

These four aspects of effectiveness (the existence of multiple models, the inevitability of change, the multidimensional character of effectiveness, and its paradoxical nature) illustrate clearly the difficulty a practitioner is likely to have in attempting to measure the success of his or her library organization. It would seem that it is more accurate to talk of "effectivenesses" than of "effectiveness" in the singular. Hrebiniak (1978) considers the implications of this for decision making within an organization, observing that the plural conveys the impression of an organization constantly being evaluated on a number of fronts, by a number of different publics. The result (or results) of these multiple and simultaneous evaluations depends on the ability of the organization and its various reference groups to make and back demands. As has already been argued, the process(es) of effectiveness(es) is/are primarily political, based on power and the use of bargaining, and not on analytical approaches to conflict resolution.

In short, the plural term "effectivenesses" serves notice that a unique decision regarding overall organizational effectiveness may never be possible. Furthermore, any summation of views will depend, ultimately, on decisions about the weights or values to be assigned to the separate evaluations of different organizational publics. Agreeing on such assignments is probably not easily done because of the vested interest and politics involved.

Hrebiniak's observations seem particularly apt in the light of the research reported here. Effectiveness is unique for each institution, and any attempt to achieve a consensus on a single model or set of criteria of effectiveness for academic libraries should be resisted.

ASSESSING LIBRARY EFFECTIVENESS

If it is neither desirable nor likely that the profession arrive at uniformly applicable models and criteria of library organizational effectiveness, how can the practitioner assess his or her library's success with any degree of confidence in the chosen methodology and tools? The research presented here suggests that the evaluator must use an instrument (or sets of instruments) that, in both design and analysis, takes into full account the highly complex nature of effectiveness. Three general observations, however, should be made to help set the context for a discussion of the form such an instrument might take.

First, as Cameron points out (1986), organizational effectiveness is mainly a problem-driven construct rather than a theory-driven construct. The basic problems facing investigators of organizational effectiveness are not theoretical problems, but are criteria problems. The most critical task facing any investigator of effectiveness is the identification of appropriate indicators and measures. Although most people have in mind some notion of what they value, those notions are frequently very difficult to operationalize.

As a result, effectiveness criteria may frequently be imposed by researchers on an organization because the criteria of real interest to the practitioner do not, as Cameron observes, easily fit into a research scheme. But the researcher's criteria may or may not be especially relevant or useful or helpful to a particular organization.

The second general observation is closely related to the first, and concerns the confusion in the use of output criteria in effectiveness assessments. This confusion involves both the failure to distinguish output data from outcome data and the failure to recognize that even outcome data do not, by themselves, adequately measure organizational effectiveness.

Outputs (here defined as the products and services created by the organization) are the dominant type of criteria used by researchers (but only recently, if popularly, in libraries). However, it is outcomes, or effects (defined as the good the organization accomplishes with its activities), that are generally used by the public in assessing an organization's worth or success.

This distinction is illustrated by Miles and Cameron (1982) in their ground-breaking study of the tobacco industry, *Coffin Nails and Corporate Strategies*, who found that in the face of a very hostile environment, tobacco companies were able to maintain a most acceptable rate of profitability and productivity. The outputs of these companies showed them to be highly successful. However, for society at large, as shown by various opinion polls, restrictive legislation, and the like, the deleterious effects of tobacco production on human health were highly important criteria in their negative assessment of the effectiveness of these companies.

It is, of course, very difficult to assess effects. Sometimes an organization's effects may be so varied and complex that it is impossible to measure them. But are outputs, by themselves, an accurate way to measure a library's success if it is the effects of library services, and their relevancy, that are the criteria which its constituencies are using to judge its worth? Of what importance is, for example, the materials availability rate or the requested materials delay, if there is little perceived relationship between those materials and learning? What do the large numbers of students who graduate having never or infrequently "used" a library with wonderful outputs suggest about their (or their instructors') perceptions of the effectiveness of the library? What do inadequate budgets or inadequate staffing suggest about an administration's perceptions of the effects of a library, which could very easily show highly acceptable outputs? Does measuring outputs, because something *has* to be measured and measuring effects is "impossible," achieve anything worthwhile? If not, why is it done?

However, it is also important to note that even the measurement of effects, alone, does not constitute an adequate measure of organizational effectiveness, because it fails to consider how or at what cost those effects were achieved. Instead, a comprehensive evaluation of effectiveness needs to encompass each of the elements in an organizational system: inputs, processes, outputs, environment, and outcomes (effects), and the relationship between them and organizational effectiveness.

A third general observation which can be made is that any test instrument designed to measure the "whole" of organizational effectiveness must recognize that effectiveness is both multivariate and multidimensional. In other words, it is not just the presence or absence of individual traits that makes a library effective or ineffective. Nor is it the cumulative presence or absence of a set of traits (as in a cumulative study of a set of scores on univariate tests). Rather, effectiveness or ineffectiveness results from the way in which the presence or absence of many traits interacts, both within an individual library and between the library and its environment.

In the research described in this book we used and tested a first-generation, prototype, measuring instrument (a questionnaire) which meets the requirements for measuring multidimensional and multivariate effectiveness. The survey used relevant criteria, including outcomes or "effects" criteria, not just those easy to quantify or to measure. All aspects of an organizational system were covered by the criteria used—inputs, processes, outputs, outcomes, and environment. All of the criteria were considered simultaneously in the measurement and analysis portions of the study. And, we would argue, the scores accumulated by individual libraries on the various domains could be considered effectiveness scores.

Should the questionnaire used in this study (and the criteria it operationalizes) now be employed to measure academic organizational effectiveness, generally? The answer is, probably no. It could be so used, but further research is needed to confirm the domains identified and to better identify the variables included in the domains and the dimensions. If different libraries were tested, would different dimensions emerge? Or would different criteria comprise similar domains?

Further research may also be needed to develop more focused multivariate measures, measures which would eventually allow libraries to do fine-grained analysis of their behavior in particular domains. These types of measures would, ideally, provide more detailed information about the variables involved, information which could then be used as librarians begin to consciously "construct" their libraries' "effectivenesses."

THE ACRL PERFORMANCE MEASURES

An interest in the measurement of library effectiveness has, of course, been both strong and ongoing. A review of the literature of library effectiveness since 1945, much of which has been noted here, confirms this observation. But along with this interest in the theoretical aspects of effectiveness, there has been a steady and increasing interest in developing simple and direct measurement tools. A recent and very striking demonstration of the persistence of this interest was the establishment, in 1984, of the Ad Hoc Committee on Performance Measures by the Association of College and Research Libraries (ACRL), and the publication, in 1990, of their manual *Measuring Academic Library Performance: A Practical Approach*. This manual, authored by Van House, Weil, and McClure and published by the American Library Association, takes a practical, how-to-do-it approach to the measurement of library performance. As an official document of the ACRL it is likely to be widely adopted and used as the instrument of choice in assessing academic library effectiveness.

The measures it includes are described in the Foreword, written by the committee, as realizing the several goals of the committee: "to present instruments or measures which could (1) measure the impact, efficiency, and effectiveness of library activities; (2) quantify or explain library output in meaningful ways to university administrators; (3) be used by heads of units to demonstrate performance levels and resource needs to library administrators; and (4) provide data useful for library planning." The committee goes on to say that the measures are also intended to be "replicable in all types of academic and research libraries, to be decision-related, to be easy and inexpensive to apply and use, to be user-oriented, and to be linked to library goals and objectives" (1990, p. vii).

The effort to produce the ACRL manual is commendable, and it does attempt to meet a felt need. Inasmuch as the measures provided are service-oriented and easy to use (their use is carefully and simply explained, all required materials are provided, and none requires a knowledge of statistics or higher math), they are likely to be well received and, as the committee states, "stimulate librarians' interest in performance measures" (1990, p. vii). As straightforward, immediately useful ways for librarians to begin to tackle the problem of assessing the activities of their organizations, they have made an important contribution. A question of some significance, then, is the relationship between the approach taken in the ACRL manual and that proposed in this research. Given its backing and the likelihood that many libraries will be looking to the manual as a way to get serious answers to serious questions (e.g., how well are we doing?), an issue of greater significance may be its relative appropriateness as a manual for assessing library effectiveness.

Even a cursory comparison of the two documents reveals what would seem to be several important differences, many of them related to differences in certain initial choices the authors made in designing their evaluation strategies. For example, in the ACRL manual an effective library is defined as "one that achieves its goals" (1990, p. 10). The authors note that there are many other ways to define effectiveness, and acknowledge some of the difficulties associated with a goal model of library effectiveness, including the often conflicting needs and demands of different constituencies which make it difficult for a library to develop a unified, prioritized set of goals. Nevertheless, the model of effectiveness on which their measures are based is a cyclical, goal-based process. In this process goals ("the standards against which performance is to be judged," p. 4) are set, criteria are developed from those goals, and measures are established to operationalize the criteria. Data are then collected, and these data are compared to the goals to assess library performance.

As has been noted throughout this book, the goal model of effectiveness may be appropriate in certain circumstances and inappropriate in others. It is important that an individual library set goals and objectives. However, doing so does not necessarily justify the use of the goal model for assessing the effectiveness of that library. In organizations where goals are (and should be) clear, measurable, time-bound, and on which there is consensus, the goal model is preferred. These conditions may hold true for a few academic libraries, but for most others they probably do not. More importantly, as noted in the earlier discussion on loose coupling, they probably should not. The uncritical use of the goal model is not likely to help librarians measure the overall effectiveness of libraries for which this model is inappropriate.

Likewise, that all libraries set goals and objectives does not justify the profession-wide adoption of the goal model for the measurement of library effectiveness. We have already argued that there probably exists today no single conceptualization of an academic library. This suggests that the profession is unlikely to come to consensus on appropriate goals for all libraries. Unfortunately, the measures offered in the ACRL manual necessarily prescribe, if not a set of *de facto* goals, at least a set of definitions of what constitutes effectiveness for various library activities. Obviously, libraries which have chosen other goals for their organizations (other definitions of effectiveness) will not find the manual useful. But this, in itself, illustrates some of the difficulties inherent in attempting to establish broadly applicable effectiveness measures using this type of approach.

Second, the measures provided in the ACRL manual address only selected areas of library performance: overall user success, including success at various library activities, overall satisfaction and ease of use; materials availability and use; facilities and equipment availability and use; and information services. Technical services are explicitly excluded, as is bibliographic instruction. The former was not included because the stated focus of the manual is service (the "quantity and quality of services delivered to users," p. ix), and not the many internal and intermediate processes in the library required to support and to deliver those services. On the other hand, bibliographic instruction, although an explicitly user-focused service, was also excluded, in this case because "evaluating instruction requires the measurement of changes in individual skills and knowledge, a different process" (p. ix) from the other measures in the manual.

That only some measures are provided would not be of concern were they not offered, in some sense, as an adequate set. Obviously the manual had to include a finite set of measures; obviously an individual library can only conduct a finite number of individual surveys and tests. But both implicitly and explicitly, these measures are offered as a way for libraries to evaluate their effectiveness (cf. p. ix, "This manual therefore presents measures that evaluate the effectiveness of library activity" and p. 8, "Similarly, the measures in this manual may be used in the self-study process for college and university accreditation to demonstrate the extent and effectiveness of the library's services").

This difference between the ACRL manual and the present work may be largely a difference in the way in which the term "effectiveness" is being used. However, confusion and imprecision in the use of language can lead to confused and incorrect applications and understandings of measurement tools. The present research has as its focus the (overall) "organizational effectiveness" of an academic library. As such, the level of analysis is explicitly identified as being that of the whole organization. In contrast, Van House and her colleagues have identified their level of analysis (p. x) as that of the library subunit (the service-unit level). "A service unit may be a single-outlet library, a branch library, or a service department. For example, in an academic library with a multi-department main library and branches around the campus, data may be collected and analyzed for each branch and for each service department in the main library (e.g., the circulation department, the reference department, the government documents department, etc.)."

The research presented in this book, however, suggests that although analysis at the subunit level can provide important information about the behavior of individual units within a library, it cannot provide a complete picture of the whole organization's effectiveness. While Van House, Weil, and McClure acknowledge the complex and multidimensional character of library effectiveness, they seem to misunderstand its significance, arguing that "a single measure assesses only one dimension of library performance" and that since multiple measures are needed to build a "more three-dimensional picture," effectiveness must be measured by a "set of measures" covering major library functions (p. 11).

In contrast, we would argue that inasmuch as many variables make up each dimension, a single dimension cannot be adequately assessed with a univariate measure. Furthermore, even using multiple univariate measures (a "set" of measures) cannot adequately assess effectiveness, since such measures do not assess the interactions among variables which are, in the end, that which gives birth to overall effectiveness.

A third important difference between the approach taken in the ACRL manual and that taken in this research is the perspective from which the assessment of effectiveness is made. Citing the movement in librarianship toward judging library effectiveness from the perspective of the user (Powell, 1988), the ACRL manual states that "the library's ultimate goal may be defined as meeting its users' information needs" (p. 11) and, consequently, assesses effectiveness from the user's perspective. In contrast, the organizational effectiveness research described here took the perspective of the library's "dominant coalition."

As Van House, Weil, and McClure point out, any difference in whose judgment on effectiveness is exercised is likely to have significant consequences for the conclusions of the study. We would argue, however, that important consequences also flow from the manner in which these perspectives are reflected in the actual design of the assessment measures. For example, in one of the measures in the ACRL manual, users are asked simply how *successful* they were, how *easy* it was to use the library, and how *satisfied* they felt after the experience. In contrast, user-related items on the questionnaire used in the study described in this book included questions relating not only to ease of use (e.g., q22, q23, q49), but also to the relevance of use to the educational purposes of the institution (e.g., q39, q58).

The issue here is not whether a user-centered perspective is appropriate for an academic library. We have argued for the centrality of the user in the development and evaluation of all library activities. Rather, the issue is how that perspective is operationalized, how the library defines its central task. We would argue that the central task of the academic library (as distinct, perhaps, from the public library) is education, not provision of information (which should be a secondary concern only). Thus, in our scheme, a *truly* user-centered perspective (as in tough love) would be operationalized in terms of skills development and would measure the sense of confidence and mastery that improving skills give students as they approach a library that is (ideally) also set up to be easy to use.

Closely related to this issue is that of the types of measures a library uses to evaluate its effectiveness. The measures offered by Van House and associates are explicitly identified as "practical output measures" (p. ix) and do not include (as the current research did) the assessment of inputs, processes, the environment, or outcomes criteria. Again, one must ask whether this is an adequate definition, if the manual intends to offer librarians a way to assess their libraries' "effectivenesses." The manual makes a strong statement about its decision ("Direct measurement of the extensiveness and effectiveness of outputs, when possible, is preferred," p. 6), but does not provide a rationale, other than to say that outcomes are difficult to measure (possibly an example of the researcher's imposing criteria on an organization more for their convenience of measurement than their relevance to the organization), and that improvement or growth in inputs or internal processes do not necessarily lead to better outputs.

Again, however, it seems to us that the real question is whether acceptable outputs alone are an adequate measure of an academic library's effectiveness, much less an adequate justification for its existence. It is true, as the committee asserts in its Foreword, that "accountability has been one of our society's major concerns in the 1980s" (p. vii). In fact, the general issue of "value added" or "educational impact" is likely to be an issue of increasing concern for librarians in the 1990s and beyond. The climate in higher education at present is one in which a wide range of constituencies— accrediting agencies, state and federal governments, parents, and students—are asking serious and pointed questions about outcomes. Are we accomplishing what we say we are accomplishing in the teaching/learning environment and is what we are accomplishing worth the effort? Librarians and their libraries and collections and services cannot be exempted from answering the questions. Nor can we merely point to our well-running libraries and say, "Look at our outstanding book availability rate and our busy bibliographic instruction program. See how effective we are." We can no longer avoid the question of how much good we are doing. It, and how well are we doing it, are together the final measures of our libraries' effectiveness.

As we have noted, no single type of effectiveness measures can be used to indicate effectiveness if effectiveness is both multivariate and multidimensional. The exclusive use of output measures is preferable to the exclusive use of input or process variables. But as this research and Cameron's have shown, the measurement of effectiveness must involve all aspects of an organization's activity, including outcomes or benefits.

Finally, one of the most striking characteristics of the ACRL manual, not matched in the present work, is its ease of use and interpretation. There is no question that real answers to real performance questions can be had, and that these real answers, if thoughtfully considered and acted upon, can be of real benefit to a library and to its users. In addition, although we have argued for the use of perceptual measures, its use of objective, rather than subjective, data may seem to many to make its approach more straightforward, more definite, more immediately useful and dependable, and, thus, more palatable to the librarian who simply wants a better library. In this, in its "immediate usability," lies one of its strengths.

But what of the seemingly large differences between these two recent efforts at helping librarians come to grips with academic library organizational effectiveness? Do they represent irreconcilably different perspectives and approaches to the issue? Can they be seen as fitting together into both a conceptual and a practical whole, which can be useful both now and as a basis for future research?

We suggest they can and offer the following observations. Organizational effectiveness is a subjective mental perception. However, the emphasis in the study of libraries and their services has been on measuring things, for example, book availability rates, volumes in the collection, etc., not mental constructs. As such it falls very much into the center of the scientific (i.e., positivistic) thinking that has dominated library "science" since World War II.

Measuring things is not wrong or irrelevant. Measuring things is important and likely to remain so as the proper and needed basis for efficiency and cost-effectiveness studies and as part of the infrastructure upon which a more informed set of dialogues, perceptions, and constructs could be based. A problem arises, however, when the differences are not clear between measuring things and measuring a construct, which are different in kind. And this problem can be acute as it becomes recognized that measuring the construct of effectiveness is important and necessary. It would be foolish to regard the measurement of a construct and the measurement of things either as equivalent or alternatives or as rivals to each other.

As with Lancaster, the measurement approaches in the ACRL manual can be useful in what Cameron has called a fine-grained analysis of dimensions. For example, the Materials Availability Survey could be used in an analysis of Dimension Three, Library Collection Adequacy, and Dimension Nineteen, Collection Physical Organization. These measures could also be used more broadly as a check on a library's performance. The effectiveness of an automobile is not determined by reading the dashboard gauges, but these instruments can tell us important things about the functioning of the engine, brakes, electrical system, and so forth. This information will not tell us if the car is designed properly for its task or if it is being employed to smuggle drugs or transport people to work. Likewise the gauges of the ACRL manual can tell practitioners some useful things about the functioning of the library. But it would be unfortunate if librarians assumed what the manual assumes, namely, that high scores on univariate performance measures necessarily indicate effectiveness.

CONCLUSION

The dilemma of academic library effectiveness continues to frustrate librarians, teaching faculty, students, and institutional administrators. As was noted in Chapter 1, there is probably no librarian, or library manager, who will not invoke effectiveness as the final unassailable criterion of the worth of his or her program, service, or organization. Buckland (1983, p. 195), again, captures this frustration:

> Although the quest for the Grail of Library Goodness has not (yet) been successful, there has been no lack of measures of performance proposed, nor of people proposing them. There have been plenty of suggestions. What is lacking is a sense of coherence—a sense of fitting together to form a whole. It is noticeable that the numerous empirical efforts need to be counterbalanced by a greater attention to theory, to context, and to how the bits and pieces fit together.

This study has attempted to begin the process of building theory for library effectiveness. The evidence presented here indicates that library effectiveness may be far more complex than any research heretofore has suggested. Nevertheless, with the insights provided by this study, it is possible to begin to see how the bits and pieces might fit together, in an empirically defensible way.

Chapter 9

LIBRARIES AND INFORMATION

The research reported in this book considered academic library effectiveness as it existed in a sampling of non–doctoral degree granting institutions of higher education near the end of the 1980s. The criteria upon which the measurement of effectiveness was based were derived from a broad variety of sources which could reasonably be expected to reflect, existentially, the transactions occurring in academic libraries for a number of years leading up to and including the period of the study. They were deliberately chosen to reflect standard practices and procedures. It is fair to call this study a "conservative" one, based as it was on mainstream and very traditional understandings of the role of a library in an academic institution.

Likewise, a cursory examination of the list of responding institutions suggests that, like most colleges and universities in the United States, these schools are largely "conservative." That is, few, if any, of these institutions would be recognized as providing "alternative" or "experimental" or broadly "innovative" educational practices on the order of St. John's College, Evergreen State College, Alverno College, or Antioch College. It is unlikely that any of the colleges in the survey would have been exerting pressure on their libraries to be anything but solidly mainstream with respect to library philosophy or practice.

But now, in the early 1990s, in the face of an unprecedented rate of change in information technologies, and under the pressure of recent expressions of national concern for and interest in the processes and products of education, we need to ask whether the traditional model for academic librarianship is still appropriate and sufficient. For example, as the "information age" has arrived on campus, its presence has become both irrevocable and troubling to campus authorities, librarians, computer and information technology specialists, and, of course, to students and faculty. The possibility of bibliographic and full-text database searching and document retrieval in offices and dorm rooms and the growing interest in the role of multimedia workstations in student learning raise the question of the adequacy of post–World War II academic library criteria as a basis for judging the effectiveness of such libraries today.

Similarly, though it has been largely ignored to date, ultimately the library cannot hope to escape its share of the intense scrutiny that has been directed at higher education in the United States. Issues such as accountability and assessment, and the cost of a college education, are debated by professionals and laypersons alike. And even private colleges and universities are no longer free from political interference, but are increasingly held responsible in the public arena for the public money that is spent in them and for the quality of the product they produce. In such a climate, it may be inevitable that the library, too, will be challenged to demonstrate what it contributes to real learning in return for the resources it consumes. And, again, those of us concerned about the measurement of library effectiveness may rightly wonder whether the perspectives and understandings which have guided library practice in the past still form an acceptable and defensible basis for giving an answer.

At this point, the reader might easily ask, if this is true, then what does it say about the research presented here, based, as it was, on these same perspectives and understandings? And what might it suggest about the assessment of library practice in the future?

In succeeding portions of this chapter, we examine a number of issues involved in the answer to these questions. Computer-based information technology is a commonplace on most campuses today, and most libraries recognize their kinship to it and the need to accept it and work with it, both as it directly affects their work and as it exists independently of the library. But is the computer merely a fast source of information and its manipulation? Are computers simply to be added to libraries to create a rich set of information tools? How successful has information technology been in the curriculum? What relationship could (or, better, should) the library and technology have to teaching and learning, which, as Evan Farber never tires of observing, are the heart of the institution, not libraries? And how, in the end, might this affect our thinking about library effectiveness and the relationship it bears to the effectiveness of a college or university?

LIBRARIES AND INFORMATION TECHNOLOGY

Historically, libraries have been the agents in colleges and universities used to acquire and manage information, or, more precisely, to acquire and manage information resources. But with the introduction of the computer and other information technologies, the library has ceased to be the exclusive information broker on campus. With this development, both administrative and academic issues related to information have become more complex. Who is to own and manage information? Where is the user of information to go, and how is he or she to learn how to appropriate and apply information in the context of a bewildering array of competing information resources? A brief story, perhaps, can illustrate the dilemma many institutions face.

> One day the Lord looked down on his creation and, tucked away in a distant corner of the earth, saw a very unhappy college president, quietly enduring the slings and arrows of outrageous fortune. But since he was obviously also long-suffering, the Lord purposed to encourage the president and came to him in his office.
>
> "My son," said the Lord, "I have noted your pain and have come to give you relief in a way appropriate for a rationalist secular humanist such as you. Ask of me three questions and I will answer you directly, unambiguously, and with complete authority. I will not direct you to study the words of Scripture, wondering which, if any, are my words and which the words of the redactor. Nor will you have to wonder if the warm glow inside of you comes from my Spirit or is the remainder of last night's pepperoni pizza. Ask now!"
>
> The president was stunned. His Bible-believing mother had told him something like this might happen some day, but here and now? Nevertheless, because he was well schooled in empirical methodologies he thought, well, why not give it a shot. This was certainly a good way to get some construct validity for the answers to the problems which were troubling him.
>
> "My Lord," he began, "Will we in higher education ever have enough money to do our jobs properly? Will we ever get Congress and the state house and corporate givers and foundations and alumni and parents to give us the money we so desperately need to do the job properly? Will we, Lord, will we?"
>
> Obviously moved by the president's emotions the Lord smiled lovingly and replied, "Yes, my son. But not in your lifetime."
>
> Getting a grip on himself, the president thought, well, I asked for it. But maybe a less self-serving question might move the Almighty to a more compassionate answer. So he asked, "Lord, will the American people ever again come to love and appreciate the work we do on their behalf? Will they yet come to understand and acknowledge how we take their grossly unprepared high school seniors and by dint of extraordinary effort turn them into thoughtful, caring young adults ready to change the world for good? Will they, Lord, will they?"
>
> The Lord was close to tears. And so he poured his heart into his answer. "Yes, my son. But not in your lifetime."
>
> It seemed as if the grand silence of the eons and of the cosmos filled the president's office. Thoroughly discouraged, but by now almost a believer, he turned once more to face the Lord and ask his final question, one that

troubled him the most, one that ate away at his confidence and sense of professionalism. "Lord," he began slowly and carefully, "Lord, will my library director and the head of my computing services ever make peace? Will they ever give up their terrible war for preferment and territory? Will they ever learn to jointly focus their efforts on large unmet student and faculty information needs? Will the unity of information and its management ever be a concept to grip their imaginations . . . for the eternal good of this campus? Will they, Lord," he implored, "Will they?" and his voice trailed off and his heart became still, waiting for the answer to such a momentous inquiry.

The Lord was moved as he had rarely been moved before. He remembered the prayers to end the bubonic plague, the fervent pleas to lift the various sieges of Jerusalem, the extraordinarily impassioned requests to bring Soviet communism to an end. But this prayer?

"Yes, my son, this too will end. But not in my lifetime."

Perhaps the reason we find the issues of information technology and access and use so complex and unwieldy is our failure to truly understand the nature of technological change. One of the enduring myths of technological innovation is that such changes are additive, that is, that each new technology merely adds to a growing rich mixture of technological possibilities and that all the previous technologies continue to be available and serve as before. But technological change is not additive; it is ecological.

Neil Postman (1991, p. 48) explains:

> What happens if we place a drop of red dye into a beaker of clear water? Do we now have clear water plus a spot of red dye? Obviously not. We have a new coloration to every molecule of water. This is what I mean by ecological change. A new medium does not add something; it changes everything. In the year 1500, after the printing press was invented, you did not have old Europe plus the printing press. You had a different Europe. After television, America was not America plus television. Television gave a new coloration to [virtually all aspects of life].
>
> This is why it is wise to be cautious about technological innovation. The consequences of technological change are always vast, often unpredictable, and largely irreversible.

Although we might raise questions about the accuracy of his science, Postman's social perspective is particularly helpful in understanding the impact of information technology on campus. With the introduction of computers into colleges and universities we do not create an information environment consisting merely of a library organization and a computer resources and services organization; rather we may be creating a significantly changed information environment.

This environment is probably considerably more than just a computerized library plus a networked campus. Although we do not yet know all the ways in which it is different, it is clear that a number of developments carry implications for libraries which are much more significant than merely additive change would suggest. Many of these carry the potential for radically altering the expectations users have of the library. For example, when faculty members conduct their own and sometimes their students' bibliographic and full-text database searching at their desks, and receive hard copy documents from sources other than their campus libraries, a fundamental change has occurred in their relationship to the library as well as in the role of the library in the institution. And this is true regardless of whether the library is brokering the service or not.

If the present information environment truly is a new entity, a genetically different thing, we may need to approach it from a distinctly different direction and to organize our use of it based on distinctly different assumptions and purposes. Most academics already recognize, for example, that neither libraries alone nor computer services alone (each as presently conceived and constituted) is fully able to meet user needs or to help faculty take full advantage of the instructional and educational possibilities inherent in this new and increasingly complex information environment. The user's actual need for information is not defined by the traditional restrictions of format or technology or even campus location that information organizations impose. Yet, all too often, in their search for and in their attempts to handle needed information, users encounter and are frustrated by organizational and physical boundaries which exist for reasons that may have little to do with how information could be, and should be, manipulated and applied.

But it is also possible that user needs cannot even be met by negotiating treaties of cooperation and collaboration between these organizations. A problem with both, in our judgment, is that each reflects ways of arranging and managing information which focus on resources rather than content. Librarians, for example, have had no real concern for information. Rather, they have been content to manipulate the resources and the physical objects bearing the information and their surrogates, typically, books, journals, and the ubiquitous catalog card. Likewise, computer specialists have been far more concerned with the machine manipulation of information than with the information itself.

The result, oversimplified, perhaps, has been the increasing isolation of both libraries and academic computing services (of both librarians and other "information" specialists) from the core issues of student learning, and, especially, how properly sequenced and integrated learning occurs in an information-rich environment. It is likely that this isolation is exacerbated as library operations become larger and more impersonal. Hugh Atkinson's reorganization of the University of Illinois libraries was based on the view (not fashionable in academic library orthodox circles) that the best library service is provided in small, special (e.g., departmental) libraries. Likewise, the success Earlham College enjoys is largely grounded in massive interpersonal contact.

In contrast, the isolation of most libraries and computer centers from the curriculum has led to the elaboration of information resource networks on campus which are organized according to historical, technological, and "professional" considerations. While these are not necessarily "bad," as such, they may be poorly matched to the way in which information is actually required and used in the classroom. Even the best efforts of a library or academic computing staff to discover what faculty and students need and want often become, in the end, well-intentioned but ultimately inadequate attempts either to "fit" user needs into an already established information structure or to "fit" that information structure into perceived user needs. In continuing to develop these services without first understanding how information is and needs to be related to teaching and learning, the responsible parties may well be organizing systems which can deal with the problems of teaching and learning only in isolated ways, in a scattershot approach.

Consider, for example, Wyatt's challenge to find 100 successful uses of information technology in teaching. Presumably the challenge came as a result of his real concern about the failure of information technologies (despite their apparent, or claimed, promise) to be more widely adopted and used. As Wyatt, chancellor of Vanderbilt University, explains, "The problem with computer technology is that this stuff is not contagious. . . . No matter how good it is, it is only used by the people who developed it and a few colleagues" ("Vanderbilt's Chancellor: A Tireless Advocate for Computer Technology," 1991).

EDUCOM, an association of computer users in higher education, took on the challenge and has, in fact, identified 101 of what they call successful classroom applications of computer technology ("Descriptions of 101 Successful Uses of Computer Technology in College Classrooms," 1991). But both the challenge and the results illustrate the problem and the inadequacy of the solution. Why isn't information technology (print and computer based) more "contagious"? And why is the EDUCOM answer not likely to trigger significant and meaningful increases in the use of these technologies?

Probably a number of reasons could be cited for what many perceive to be the "underutilization" of computer-based technologies on campus. Among these might be apathy and lack of initiative among professors unwilling to change their teaching methods, lack of knowledge about potentially useful software and hardware, and, all too commonly, the unavailability of these resources. But however real these problems might be, one wonders if the fundamental reason these technologies are not more fully exploited is that thinking faculty understand that integration of information technologies into the classroom is not—ultimately—the issue (McDonald and Micikas, 1992).

Rather, the core issue is student learning: how learning occurs, how learning is related to information, and how consistently meaningful interaction between the learner and information can be most effectively facilitated. And faculty also understand that this issue is not—ultimately—addressed by substituting a computer-based drill for flash cards here or by introducing computer-based simulations to supplement actual laboratory sessions there. At heart, learning is and always will be a curricular and pedagogical matter, a matter of the overall structure of the learning and teaching environment, and of the quality of interaction which the learning task creates between the learner and information. And, as such, it probably cannot be adequately addressed by information specialists (or even by faculty) operating at the level of the individual computer or information application.

It is no doubt true that the questions of how students learn and how students can be helped to learn have been very much at the heart of the development of the best of the individually successful computer-based and information technology–based projects. (It is also no doubt true that these issues have been given no more than lip service in the development of many others.) But learning comes about *whenever* the student is productively "engaged" with information; the medium or the mechanism through which that is accomplished is not, fundamentally, the issue. It may be true that computer-based and library-based projects can sometimes help bring about that engagement, but they do not do so as an automatic result of their nature. Nor is it true that the required engagement of learner with task, of learner with information, cannot be brought about through other media or other mechanisms. Information resources—libraries and computers—are just additional tools that the talented teacher can use to bring about that engagement. Neither, in the end, can make up for poor teaching. Nor is either required to make the talented teacher effective.

Likewise, learning is not simply an issue of the individual learning experience. Rather, it results from the totality of those experiences, properly structured and sequenced and coordinated. Even using the best projects possible, it is not likely that one or two individually successful activities or learning experiences will significantly change a student's overall achievement or development in college. It is even unlikely that many such projects—strung together as they tend to be without coherence or logic or intellectual sequence— will have the needed effect. It may be, in fact, that until the role of information itself in student learning is better understood and better articulated, the use of technology-based activities as such, however interesting and individually successful some might be, will not have a meaningful or a broad impact on the way in which education is accomplished—or attempted—on college and university campuses.

It is significant in this regard that Wyatt's challenge to the information resources community was not to identify 100 teaching and learning problems for which technological solutions might be appropriate (in that case real learning needs would be driving the use of technology). Rather, the challenge was to find 100 examples of ways in which information technology—looking for work, as it were—was able to find itself employed in odd jobs around academia. Likewise, although the EDUCOM list of projects reveals what are undoubtedly a number of useful applications of technology for teaching, we feel compelled to ask to what extent isolated and piecemeal implementation of such projects will significantly increase overall student learning, or will noticeably strengthen and enhance the total education a student receives. Just because technology can do something does not mean that that is the best way to do it or that it should be done at all.

The question of how broad our thinking about student interaction with information may need to be is addressed in the next section. But it is entirely possible—likely, even—that the traditional model of information provision on campus (the traditional model of an academic library), even with the introduction of the computer into it, will not be able to be molded, or twisted, or enhanced sufficiently to survive the growing demands that today's information users will place on it.

Instead, perhaps the existence and elaboration of information technology (print and machine readable) need to emerge (be generalized) from a fundamental understanding of how information itself is involved in teaching and learning. That is, perhaps, we can no longer afford a resource-based approach. Certainly, few would argue that it should be developed and expanded simply because information resources and technology exist *sui generis*, and must be supported by tuition dollars regardless of the work they do.

INFORMATION TECHNOLOGY AND THE CURRICULUM

The present concern for assessment and accountability in higher education also raises questions about the activities and services of the academic library. What contribution does the library make to "real" and "active" student learning? And what implications might this have for how library effectiveness is understood and measured?

One does not have to look far to find an obvious answer to the first question. The exponential growth of knowledge and the introduction of information technology onto college campuses have not only presented technological and organizational problems to institutions of higher education but also philosophical and educational challenges with which they are frequently hard pressed to deal. As the information base increases, and as the useful life of that information decreases, faculty are becoming more and more aware of the need to help students become learners in their own right, capable of independently seeking and acquiring information to expand and to replenish that which was gained in the classroom. Likewise, as new information technologies are introduced, and as new ways of using these technologies are developed, librarians and faculty alike are becoming more concerned that students be given appropriate opportunities to develop the intellectual and technical skills required to exploit their potential.

But how are these objectives to be realized? What can institutions do to encourage their students to become truly "active" and "independent" and "lifelong" learners? How will institutions make sure that students graduate with current and useful information skills? Should the library have anything to do with the development of these skills? And to what degree, if any, should computer and information technology specialists be concerned with them?

We are neither the first, nor the only, educators and librarians concerned enough about student learning to raise such questions. In fact, the role of the library in student learning has been debated in the library literature for decades (Branscomb, 1940; Knapp, 1966; Beaubien, Hogan, and George, 1982; Mellon, 1987). A recent and very influential expression of such concerns is the book *Information Literacy: Revolution in the Library* by Patricia Senn Breivik and E. Gordon Gee (1989). Their appeal to college administrators, to faculty, and to librarians points out the enormous implications of our collective unwillingness or inability to prepare our young people adequately to face the challenges of surviving in a world in which information and the ability to locate and use it have become increasingly important and valuable commodities. It argues that we need to expand the current definition of the term "literacy" to include the ability to access and evaluate information for a particular need.

An important element of Breivik and Gee's answer to the challenges of the information age is what they call "the introduction of library-based learning into the curriculum" (1989, p. 37). Essentially, their position is that good learning is active and individualized, and that good learning experiences imitate reality, accommodate a constantly changing information base, are responsive to a variety of learning styles, and are best developed within a nonthreatening environment. "Only when classroom instructors and librarians cooperate in shifting the focus toward library-based learning will these six elements of a good learning experience come together in undergraduate education. A shared campus vision of the implications of the information age and a corresponding statement of educational philosophy . . . are important steps in promoting such cooperation" (p. 39).

However attractive these ideas may appear on the surface, we wonder if they do not still miss the point. Information literacy, in its full sense (as the ability to acquire, evaluate, and use information), is not exclusively, or even largely, developed in the library or by completing so-called library-based assignments. It is actually developed (or not, as the case may be) as a result of all of the learning activities the student experiences while in school.

At issue here is a distinction between "information literacy" as a library-based problem needing a library-based solution and "information literacy" as a pedagogical and curricular problem needing pedagogical and curricular solutions. This difference is easily illustrated by the simple observation that all of what a student does in college involves interaction with information. All that separates a lecture-based or a textbook-based assignment from a library-based assignment is the relative proximity of the information. Yes, accessing the information located in the library may require a few additional skills. But in an age when information can be bought at will and in which the easy accessibility of information is becoming increasingly a commonplace, these skills are not, ultimately, the really crucial ones. Instead, what counts is the student's ability to recognize when information is needed, to evaluate the available information, and to select and apply that which is useful and relevant. And, presumably, these are the same skills that are practiced in all other assignments and learning activities the student is called upon to complete.

In fact, it may be that the issues of "information literacy" are, actually, issues of "active learning" (how students learn to acquire, evaluate, and apply information in the completion of a task, the solution of a problem, or the making of a decision). That is, helping students become "information literate" is not a way to helping them become "active learners." Rather, "active learning" means becoming information literate. If this is true, then the issues of information literacy are not library or information technology issues, as such, but are, again, pedagogical and curricular issues. They have to do with what the student needs to learn and how, and what teachers will teach and how.

And as such, they may need to be addressed not by librarians or information specialists, but by the faculty themselves. However much a good bibliographic instruction program (or a good information-seeking skills program) might help learning be more active, it may still be a subtle case of information technology—in this case, libraries—looking for work. All too often and all too easily, library assignments are perceived as being artificially added onto courses in order to get students to learn to use this resource. "Real" information-based assignments, in contrast, flow from the real needs to know which are a natural and central part of the practice of any discipline. As Carmen Schmersahl points out in her article on teaching library research as a process, not a product (Schmersahl, 1987, p. 232), "We can more profitably teach our students to use library research if, rather than separating the activity out as relevant only for the writing of the research paper, we teach research as part of the recursive generative process of writing and so encourage students to see that doing research, whether in the library, the laboratory, or the 'real world,' is also a recursive process of discovery."

The core issue, then, which faces college administrators, faculty, librarians, and computer specialists is not the information resources themselves (as traditional information and library science would argue), but the information they contain and how that and all other information is identified, retrieved, evaluated, and applied in answering questions, in completing tasks, and in solving problems. The issue is not who will own and manage formal information resources, nor even how they will be organized and made accessible to potential users, but how those users will learn when and for what purposes they need information of all sorts, and how they will learn to use it. This issue transcends the library or the academic computing lab; it even transcends the bounds of any individual classroom. In fact, it is a curricular issue, flowing directly from questions of what our students need to learn and how we will teach it. And that teaching and learning must occur, not within the essentially false and artificial bounds of a library, or even of a library plus computers, but within the real, rich, complex information climate in which our students live now and will need to live and function as they leave our campuses to practice their disciplines.

If this is true, as we abandon attempts to force technology and libraries into the curriculum, and as we allow pedagogical and learning issues to determine the character and shape of our libraries and our information technology organizations (just as pedagogical and learning issues determine the shape and character of the curriculum), it is likely that they both will become organizations quite different from what they are now.

For example, one model for library and information services which, we believe, offers a very good possibility for integrating information with the curriculum is the "cultural legitimacy" model discussed by Weigand (1986) and Robbins (1991). In this model, the "professional" concern for information ceases to be located in the library and shifts to the institution's academic divisions and departments. Workers operating libraries are called, using Robbins's terminology, "library engineers" or "library custodians," and their responsibilities are focused exclusively on collection control: inventory, warehousing, materials storage, and distribution. Intellectual access is not their concern. Rather, the duties associated with intellectual access will be performed by "information professionals," that is, credentialed faculty from within the various teaching departments who have developed an information expertise. Robbins (1991, p. 215) explains:

> It seems reasonable to surmise that information professionals hired by campus units would first be required to be of that work unit, e.g., bonafide sociologists, budget analysts, mechanical engineers, [etc.]. Such information professionals would then posses that essential quality . . . [of] cultural au-

> thority. This cultural authority . . . is the recognized authority to determine what records contain those definitions of reality and judgements of meaning and value that are considered valid and true.
>
> Only those educated in the traditions, approaches, and paradigms of a field can be recognized as possessing cultural authority; thus, only similarly trained colleagues will be recognized as legitimate information providers/partners in the intellectual workplace. Those working in the information arena without benefit of subject qualification will never obtain colleague status; they will remain uninitiated staff servants rather than intellectual partners. The growing complexity of the information access menu and the importance of timely retrieval of appropriate information to the research, teaching, and development, and service enterprise of the university requires the creation of a class of culturally authoritative information partners.

Robbins indicates that the training of such information professionals would be integrated with the preparation of practitioners in the various disciplines, as a speciality of that discipline. And then, alluding to "the present, somewhat disturbing winnowing, without any apparent prior sifting, in educational programs of library and information studies" (p. 215), she strongly suggests that faculties of schools of library and information studies ought to make common cause with colleagues in other departments, "in order to rethink the mission, goals, and objectives for the education of information professionals in academia . . . [and] to aid in the development of educational program planning that will best fill the need for providing the most effective information access and delivery on campus."

Operationalizing such ideas would in no way diminish the academic importance or value of the library. Instead, it would allow a library to be truly a library and release it from the burden of pretending it was a teaching department. It would also free libraries to concentrate on finding simpler and better ways to provide bibliographic and physical access to print and machine-readable information resources, a longing close to the heart of scholars.

At a recent meeting of the American Council of Learned Societies those attending noted several ways *they*, not necessarily librarians, would like access to information enhanced (Greenberg, 1991). Leading the list was affordable online bibliographies that contained standardized information on current and past periodicals. They also wanted *true* cooperative collecting of periodicals and monographs by colleges and universities, coupled with a universal interlibrary loan system. Likewise, they strongly urged the development of machine-readable full-text versions of the existing journal literature. Greenberg (1991) notes: "All of these items are part of a system whose parts are closely interrelated. *We need to think about the methods and costs of changing an entire system of information access and delivery, not just about changing individual pieces of the system* [emphasis supplied]."

This is one example of what might happen to libraries if we were to allow their character and structure to flow from teaching and learning, instead of forcing the present library model *into* teaching and learning. Whatever the model that eventually obtains, it is our conviction that we can no longer afford to perpetuate the artificial boundaries that exist between libraries and the classroom. Ideally these distinctions should never have existed. Perhaps the historical need to house more and more volumes, and with that need the requirement for a large building, led naturally enough to thinking of library information as something different from other information. Technology, however, is destroying those walls and helping us to understand libraries as a process. As we increasingly understand what it means for a library to be process, not place, we will be discovering what it means to integrate information into the curriculum and to understand this integration as the curriculum using information, not the library insisting on being used.

CHANGING LIBRARIES AND THEIR EFFECTIVENESS

In the evolving information and instructional environment on campus, the question is not whether libraries will change. Rather the issue is how libraries will change and how they will be recognized as effective ones during, perhaps, a protracted period of transition. And just as importantly, how will they subsequently measure their effectiveness as organizations different from earlier classic academic libraries and needing to employ criteria on which there may not be wide "professional" consensus?

One could assert, presumably, that during a period of transition we should abandon the idea of effectiveness and focus instead on some form of pragmatic management that would get libraries through to whatever their new missions and structures might be. Although, there is a certain appeal in such a position (after all, why try to make effective what is merely transitory?), it ignores the realities of organizational transformation and the need to manage change. A fundamental objective of assessment is to know where one is, to be sure that one is travelling in the right direction. It is during periods of change and transition, perhaps, when organizations (and their constituents) need most to be sure that they are effective ones, especially if they wish to remain in charge of that change.

But change is not likely to occur in all academic libraries at the same time and at the same speed. It is easy to imagine a situation (partly because it is already occurring) in which many of the colleges and universities in the United States would be, with respect to the management of their academic information resources and services, in many different places, some stoutly defending the structures of classic, traditional librarianship, decrying the very existence of "information," others waffling or muddling along, waiting to see what the "leaders" will do and what the foundations will fund, and yet others, moving boldly (and, perhaps, mistakenly) into new patterns of academic information management and applications.

How will such disparate organizations, each focused on information management and service, assess their effectiveness? It is our conviction that how we assess reflects our conception of excellence. In an address to the faculties and administrators of Pepperdine University (October 26, 1991), Alexander "Sandy" Astin, professor of education and director of the Higher Education Research Institute, University of California, Los Angeles, and recognized as a highly respected authority on assessment in higher education in the United States, noted that there are, fundamentally, three assessment methods in colleges and universities: (1) reputational, (2) resources, and (3) talent development.

In higher education, Astin maintained, our preferred method of assessment, the reputational, is flawed because it is "normative" and requires that there be winners and losers, institutional and student. Losers are those rated average or worse. Who or what organization wishes to be called average? Furthermore, normative assessment is artificial; it does not relate to reality. The results of normative measurements are a product of the assessment method. Likewise, the resources model, with its focus on attainments and possessions, is flawed because it is measuring the wrong things. Money, endowments, expenditures, student/faculty ratios, the test scores of entering freshmen may contribute to an institution's effectiveness, but these things cannot, of themselves, be the measures of our success. Rather, they feed the reputational assessment which in turn creates a demand for more resources in order to keep the assessment of reputation high.

Instead, Astin continued, a college or university, and its constituent parts, can only legitimately assess itself on how effectively it develops the talents of its students, which, of course, is the core of outcomes measurement, and is the method most consistent with the educational mission of higher education. To be sure, Astin further maintained, there are several sources of data for assessing our effectiveness in talent development. Inputs, processes and environmental experiences, and outputs all contribute to the effectiveness of our organizations in producing the desired outcome: talent development. In the end, however, it is the outcomes we value which we choose to assess. And it is those values which lie at the heart of the assessment process.

We believe that the institution-specific, dimensionalized model of effectiveness presented in this book is likely to be a much more successful one for measuring the effectiveness of "libraries" during a period of transition than the historic univariate or multivariate static models described in Chapters 1 and 2. It allows each information organization to be seen as effective in relationship to the strategic choices it or its host institution may have made. It enables each organization to be recognized as effective regardless of the kind of (successful) activity carried on in similar or analogous information organizations. It allows each institution to engineer this effectiveness as it moves toward goals which may require continuing change in its library or other kinds of information control and service. And, most importantly, it allows each evolving organization, regardless of its place on the change continuum, to focus its efforts on the outcome: developed, educated students.

Beyond its ability to allow changing organizations to monitor their effectiveness, the dimensionalized, organization-specific approach to effectiveness measurement is well suited to whatever form or forms of information management develop on campus. Whether that form is a continuing traditional library or a library which has yielded its responsibilities in the teaching and learning environment to the academic departments or one in which all information resources are combined, regardless of academic focus, or one whose structure is not yet understood, the ability of the organization's stakeholders to choose criteria existentially, to measure its effectiveness subjectively but with empirical verification, without reference to external demands or standards on which, perhaps, there is no consensus, will be a considerable advantage.

What do we, academic librarians at the end of the twentieth century, value? For virtually the entire existence of our profession, we equated our possessions with effectiveness. Books, budgets, and beatitudes governed our organizations. More recently, we supposed that our operations and processes were the keys to effectiveness. Lately, we have measured the success of our organizational work for our users and called such assessment, effectiveness. It is true, as we have seen, many of the inputs, processes, outputs, and the environments of our libraries contribute to their success. But very few of us (Johnson, Branscomb, Knapp, Farber, Breivik, and not too many more) ever seemed to have understood that ultimately the only effectiveness criterion that truly matters is the developed, educated student. Without successful students, successful libraries are meaningless. What do we truly value?

Appendix 1

EFFECTIVENESS CRITERIA

The following are the criteria from which the questionnaire was developed. These were derived from the literature search, from the researcher's experience, and from comments of respondents to the questionnaire pretest. The criteria are grouped by organizational aspect. Each criterion is followed by the number of the question or questions assessing the criterion. Criteria added or modified after the pretest are indicated by an asterisk.

ENVIRONMENT:

1. The library acquires sufficient personnel and material resources from the college to support its programs and services. Questions 1, 2, 3
2. The college supports innovation in library services and activities. Question 4
3. The library supports the mission and goals of the college. Question 62
4. The library is responsive to the requirements of the college's educational programs and curricula. Question 64
5. The library is a member of and actively participates in appropriate formal bibliographic and library service cooperatives. Question 67
6. The library maintains informal cooperative relationships with neighboring college, high school, and public libraries. Questions 70, 71, 72
7. Librarians actively promote the spiritual, cultural, and social life of the college. Questions 63, 87
8. The college's faculty actively supports the library's programs and services. Question 5
9. Librarians and teaching faculty interact as professional colleagues in the pursuit of the college's academic objectives. Question 33

INPUTS:

1. The library's budget recommendations are developed with the participation of the librarians. Question 68
2. The library's budget, approved by the college's administration, is based on recommendations of the library's director. Question 34
3. The librarians are involved in decisions regarding the expenditure of budgeted funds. Question 69
4. The library director has the responsibility and authority for the expenditure of budgeted funds. Question 35
5. The facilities are adequate for the library's tasks and users' requirements. Questions 14, 15
6. The library provides furniture and equipment sufficient to meet its own task requirements and those of its users. Questions 16, 17
7. *The size of the existing collection is large enough to meet the needs of the library's users. Question 11
8. *The existing collection *contains* materials of sufficient quality to support the emphases of the college's academic programs and curricula. Questions 6, 7
9. Quality of the collection is judged by comparison with lists of key literature, professional assessments by librarians, and judgment by qualified faculty. Questions 73, 74, 75
10. *The library's collections provide most of the materials users require. Question 27
11. Materials are physically organized in such a way that they are readily accessible and space is efficiently used. Questions 20, 21, 22
12. The most heavily used materials are stored in the most accessible locations. Question 23
13. The card catalog accurately and consistently represents the contents of the library's collections. Questions 40, 81
14. The library's cataloging system is easily understood and used by faculty and students. Question 49
15. *The library has a collection development plan which is responsive to changes in the curricula and patterns of library use. Questions 38, 39
16. Librarians, faculty, and students participate in the selection of library materials. Questions 48, 65, 66, 85, 86
17. *The library annually *acquires* materials in sufficient *quantity* to support the needs of its users. Question 12
18. *The library annually *acquires* materials of sufficient *quality* to support the emphases of the college's academic programs and curricula. Questions 9, 10
19. *The library acquires information materials to meet future needs of the institution's academic programs and curricula. Question 59

20. The library acquires materials which support the research activities of the faculty. Question 13
21. Materials purchased reflect the variety of forms in which information is presented or distributed. Question 8

PROCESSES:

1. Library goals are explicitly stated. Question 28
2. Library goals are agreed upon by college management, librarians, and users. Questions 29, 30
3. Library policies and managerial decision making are the joint responsibility of librarians and library administrators. Question 41
4. Organizational management techniques are used in the administration of the library. Question 37
5. The size and diversity of the staff is adequate to meet the requirements of the library. Questions 31, 32
6. Library job descriptions include a detailed statement of actual activities, indicating the importance of each activity, the conditions under which the job is performed, and the materials needed to carry out the job. Questions 42, 88
7. Librarians are considered members of the college's faculty. Question 80, 95
8. Professional staff have a minimum of a master's degree in library or information science from an ALA accredited school. Question 94
9. The librarians are skilled in the application of professional knowledge to solve specific problems and to attain specific goal objectives. Questions 18, 36, 83
10. Librarians are trained in the use of computer-based information management and dissemination. Question 84
11. Librarians and clerical staff are provided with training by the library for their assigned tasks. Question 43
12. *The library provides appropriate opportunities and rewards for professional development. Question 19
13. Professional and clerical staff pursue opportunities for continuing education. Questions 92, 93
14. Librarians are involved in the activities of appropriate professional societies. Questions 90, 91
15. Salaries, wages, and fringe benefits are commensurate with those paid to employees of comparable institutions. Question 60
16. The library maintains mechanisms for regular communication between library staff and management and between the library and its users. Question 78
17. Personnel recommendations and decisions affecting librarians are made on the basis of evaluations by peer librarians and library administrators. Questions 44, 89

18. Clerical staff are regularly evaluated by immediate supervisors and/or library administrators. Question 45
19. Librarians and clerical staff exhibit a high degree of morale. Questions 46, 47

OUTPUTS:

1. The library develops innovative ways to perform its tasks and services. Question 77
2. The library publicizes its services so that users know they exist. Question 24
3. *The library maintains mechanisms for regular communication with its users. Question 79
4. Students and faculty make regular use of library materials and services. Questions 25, 26
5. The library staff provide prompt, courteous, and consistently reliable service. Question 57
6. Librarians are available to advise users in ways to find information, and to assist them when appropriate. Question 53, 55
7. Librarians are involved in formal efforts to teach information-seeking skills. Question 56
8. The library provides sufficient indexing and abstracting material to enable the user to identify most of the material required to meet his information needs regardless of its location on or off campus. Question 50
9. The library provides machine-readable bibliographic database searching as required or as needed. Question 54
10. The library maintains a system to control and account for borrowing activity. Question 61
11. The library maintains a collection of materials reserved for use primarily within the library and for a limited amount of time. Question 82
12. The library maintains a readily available system for obtaining in a timely manner materials which users require but which are not owned by the library. Question 51, 52
13. The library evaluates its services and programs regularly. Question 76
14. The college perceives the library's programs and services as having a highly positive effect on student academic growth and development. Question 58

Appendix 2

QUESTIONNAIRE, ACADEMIC LIBRARY EFFECTIVENESS STUDY, SEPTEMBER 1986

TO: Participants, Academic Library Effectiveness Study

FROM: Joseph McDonald, Doctoral Candidate, Drexel University and Director of Library Services, Holy Family College

This questionnaire asks you to rate *your perceptions* of the presence and strength, *in your library*, of a number of factors which a large survey of library-related literature suggests contribute to library organizational-level effectiveness.

Please make an effort to answer every question, even if you must estimate. The key concern is your *perception* of these factors in your library. On the last page you are asked to mark the one "generic" title which most closely describes your own title or major set of responsibilities. This is very important for analysis purposes only. *No* individual or library will *ever* be identified in any report on the study. TOTAL CONFIDENTIALITY OF ALL RESPONSES IS ASSURED, ABSOLUTELY.

Please return the questionnaire in the enclosed postage-paid envelope within two weeks of the time you receive it. Your time and participation is truly appreciated and a copy of the summary of the study's findings and conclusions is yours by simply checking the last line on the last page.

QUESTIONNAIRE	DESCRIPTIVE STATISTICS
Library environments can be rated according to their "richness" or "leanness". Please rate the following resources in this library's environment in terms of whether the resource present in the environment is more than adequate, adequate, or inadequate.	Descriptive statistics for each question in the final questionnaire are shown below. V=variance; M=missing (N and percent); ME=mean; S.D.=standard deviation.*

	More Than Adequate (rich)		Adequate		Inadequate (lean)			V	M	ME	S.D.
1. Annual Budget	7	6	5	4	3	2	1	1.777	3 (0.8%)	3.517	1.333
2. Professional Staff	7	6	5	4	3	2	1	2.120	4 (1.0%)	3.658	1.456
3. Clerical Staff	7	6	5	4	3	2	1	1.742	5 (1.3%)	3.472	1.320
4. College Support for Library Innovation	7	6	5	4	3	2	1	2.475	4 (1.0%)	3.874	1.573
5. Faculty Support for Library Programs and Services	7	6	5	4	3	2	1	1.820	5 (1.3%)	4.106	1.349

To what extent are the following characteristics typical of this library. Please enter the appropriate number using the scale immediately below.

Very True or Highly Typical of This Library			Neither Typical nor Atypical		Very Untrue or Highly Atypical of This Library	
7	6	5	4	3	2	1

	V	M	ME	S.D.
_____6. The existing collection contains materials of sufficient breadth and depth to support the emphases of the college's curricula.	1.754	----	5.021	1.324
_____7. The existing collection contains materials of sufficient currency to support the emphases of the college's curricula.	1.898	----	4.802	1.378

*The range for each question = 6.

Very True or Highly Typical of This Library		Neither Typical nor Atypical			Very Untrue or Highly Atypical of This Library		V	M	ME	S.D.
7	6	5	4	3	2	1				

	V	M	ME	S.D.
_____8. Materials purchased represent the variety of forms in which information is presented or distributed.	2.346	----	4.893	1.532
_____9. The library annually acquires materials of sufficient breadth and depth to support the emphases of the college's curricula.	1.954	----	4.768	1.398
_____10.The library annually acquires materials of sufficient currency to support the emphases of the college's curricula.	1.870	----	4.888	1.367
_____11.The size of the library's collection is large enough to meet the learning and teaching needs of the users.	2.086	1 (0.3%)	4.911	1.444
_____12. The library annually acquires materials in sufficient quantity to support the learning and teaching needs of its users.	1.844	9 (2.3%)	4.605	1.358
_____13. The library annually acquires materials which support the research activities of the faculty.	2.095	9 (2.3%)	3.528	1.447
_____14. Facilities are adequate for the library's tasks.	3.039	9 (2.3%)	4.160	1.743
_____15. Facilities are adequate for the library users' requirements.	2.859	11 (2.9%)	4.308	1.591
_____16. Furniture and equipment are sufficient to meet the library's task requirements.	2.786	11 (2.9%)	4.276	1.669
_____17. Furniture and equipment are sufficient to meet the library users' requirements.	2.863	9 (2.3%)	4.288	1.692

Very True or Highly Typical of This Library		Neither Typical nor Atypical			Very Untrue or Highly Atypical of This Library		V	M	ME	S.D.
7	6	5	4	3	2	1				

	V	M	ME	S.D.
____18. Librarians are appointed to positions that match their education and experience with the nature and scope of their responsibilities.	1.594	10 (2.5%)	5.447	1.262
____19. The library provides appropriate opportunities and rewards for professional development.	2.365	11 (2.9%)	4.271	1.538
____20. Sufficient space is provided to shelve all of the library's collections.	3.628	9 (2.3%)	4.019	1.905
____21. Space for shelving and storage is efficiently used.	1.690	9 (2.3%)	5.432	1.300
____22. Materials are physically organized so that they are readily accessible.	1.734	9 (2.3%)	5.440	1.317
____23. Most heavily used materials are shelved in the most accessible locations.	1.797	15 (3.9%)	5.100	1.341
____24. The library publicizes its services so that users know they exist.	1.642	9 (2.3%)	4.808	1.281
____25. Students make regular use of library materials and services.	1.583	9 (2.3%)	4.989	1.258
____26. Faculty make regular use of library materials and services.	1.776	9 (2.3%)	4.341	1.333
____27. Library users are usually able to secure the materials they require from the library's collections.	1.263	9 (2.3%)	4.808	1.124
____28. Library goals and objectives are explicitly stated.	2.736	9 (2.3%)	4.829	1.654

Very True or Highly Typical of This Library		Neither Typical nor Atypical			Very Untrue or Highly Atypical of This Library		V	M	ME	S.D.
7	6	5	4	3	2	1				

	V	M	ME	S.D.
_____29. Library goals and objectives are agreed upon by library management and librarians.	2.855	9 (2.3%)	5.016	1.690
_____30. Consistent efforts are made to secure input from library users in the development of library goals and objectives.	2.192	9 (2.3%)	3.979	1.481
_____31. The library staff is large enough to accomplish the work of the library in a reasonably expeditious manner.	2.609	9 (2.3%)	4.027	1.615
_____32. The library staff has people with a sufficient diversity of skills to do all the work which needs to be done.	1.949	9 (2.3%)	4.883	1.396
_____33. Librarians and teaching faculty interact as professional colleagues in the pursuit of the college's academic objectives.	2.171	10 (2.6%)	4.834	1.473

This section asks you to rate your perceptions of the general functioning of the library. Please respond by circling the number that best represents your perception of each item.

How Do You Perceive the Following?

34. Library Budget

			V	M	ME	S.D.
The approved budget is very close to the director's recommendations	7 6 5 4 3 2 1	The approved budget is developed by the college with very little input from the director	2.696	15 (3.9%)	4.512	1.642

35. <u>Responsibility for Budget Expenditures</u>			V	M	ME	S.D.
Library director is solely responsible for expenditure of budgeted funds; requires no prior institutional approval	7 6 5 4 3 2 1	Library director cannot expend any budgeted funds without prior college approval	2.871	15 (3.9%)	5.035	1.694

36. <u>Application of Professional Skills</u>			V	M	ME	S.D.
Librarians in <u>this library</u> are highly skilled in the application of professional knowledge to the solution of specific problems and in the attainment of goals and objectives	7 6 5 4 3 2 1	Librarians on this staff are ineffective in solving specific problems and reaching goals and objectives	1.011	3 (0.8%)	5.554	1.005

37. <u>Library Management</u>			V	M	ME	S.D.
Organizational management techniques are consciously used in the administration of the library	7 6 5 4 3 2 1	The library is directed informally with little use of accepted management or supervisory principles	2.338	2 (0.5%)	4.542	1.529

38. <u>Collection Development</u>			V	M	ME	S.D.
The library's collection development is well-planned and carefully monitored	7 6 5 4 3 2 1	Library collection is unplanned and haphazard	1.989	2 (0.5%)	4.895	1.410

39. <u>Collection Development</u>			V	M	ME	S.D.
A strong effort is made in this library to develop its collections in response to changes in the curriculum and patterns of collection use	7 6 5 4 3 2 1	Little effort is made in this library to so develop its collections	1.536	2 (0.5%)	5.531	1.239

Item	Scale	Opposite	V	M	ME	S.D.
40. Card Catalog						
The catalog (in card or any other form) accurately and consistently represents the contents of the library's collections	7 6 5 4 3 2 1	The catalog is incomplete and contains many errors	1.572	3 (0.8%)	5.567	1.254
41. Policies and Decisions						
Library policies and managerial decision-making are the joint responsibility of librarians and library administrators	7 6 5 4 3 2 1	Policies and decisions are made unilaterally by the chief library administrator	2.651	4 (0.8%)	4.976	1.628
42. Job Descriptions (If there are no written job descriptions in your library, please do not answer this question.)						
Written job descriptions are precise and complete	7 6 5 4 3 2 1	Written job descriptions are vague or incomplete	2.054	84 (21.9%)	5.200	1.433
43. Staff Training						
The Library provides librarians and clerical staff with the opportunities to receive all the training required for their assignments	7 6 5 4 3 2 1	Library provides no such opportunities	1.692	4 (1.0%)	5.084	1.301
44. Evaluation Of Librarians						
Evaluation by both peers and library administration is the basis for personnel recommendations affecting librarians	7 6 5 4 3 2 1	The chief library administrator unilaterally makes personnel recommen datios	3.775	9 (2.3%)	4.499	1.943
45. Clerical Staff Evaluation						
Clerical staff are regularly evaluated by their immediate supervisors and /or library administrators	7 6 5 4 3 2 1	Clerical staff do not not receive regular performance evaluations	3.763	5 (1.3%)	5.216	1.940

			V	M	ME	S.D.
46. Staff Morale						
Clerical staff exhibit a positive and optimistic spirit with regard to their work	7 6 5 4 3 2 1	Clerical staff are dispirited and pessimistic about their work	2.038	6 (1.6%)	4.810	1.428
47. Staff Morale						
Librarians exhibit a positive and optimistic spirit with regard to their work	7 6 5 4 3 2 1	Librarians are dispirited and pessimistic about their work	1.989	3 (0.8%)	5.005	1.410
48. Selection of Materials						
Students are consistently involved in the selection of library materials	7 6 5 4 3 2 1	Students are not involved in the selection of library materials	1.733	4 (1.0%)	2.474	1.316

Please rate the services of this library on the following scales. Circle the appropriate number.

			V	M	ME	S.D.
49. The library's cataloging system is easily understood and used by faculty and students	7 6 5 4 3 2 1	The cataloging system is difficult to understand and use	1.689	5 (1.3%)	5.142	1.299
50. The library provides sufficient indexing and abstracting material to enable the user to identify most of the material required to meet his information needs regardless of it's location on or off campus	7 6 5 4 3 2 1	Library supplied bibliographic materials are not sufficient	.956	5 (1.3%)	5.726	.987
51. The library maintains a formal and well publicized interlibrary loan service	7 6 5 4 3 2 1	The library does not maintain a formal interlibrary loan service	1.454	5 (1.3%)	5.860	1.206

			V	M	ME	S.D.
52. Users are able to obtain promptly materials which are not owned by the library (regardless of the method employed)	7 6 5 4 3 2 1	Materials not owned by the library are obtained only after long delays	1.460	6 (1.6%)	5.503	1.208
53. A librarian is always available to help users	7 6 5 4 3 2 1	Users frequently are not able to find a librarian to help them	1.727	4 (1.0%)	5.461	1.314
54. Machine-readable biblio-graphic database search-ing is easily obtained in or through the library	7 6 5 4 3 2 1	Database searching is not available	3.274	4 (1.0%)	5.247	1.809
55. Librarians provide infor-mal guidance in the use of the library and its materials	7 6 5 4 3 2 1	Librarians do not provide such guidance	.631	4 (1.0%)	6.295	.794
56. Librarians are involved in formal efforts to teach students information seeking skills	7 6 5 4 3 2 1	Librarians are not involved in such efforts	1.623	4 (1.0%)	5.992	1.274
57. Library staff provide prompt, courteous, and consistently reliable service	7 6 5 4 3 2 1	Library staff service is slow, grudging and unreliable	.758	4 (1.0%)	6.042	.871
58. The college perceives the library's programs and services as having a highly positive effect on student academic growth and development	7 6 5 4 3 2 1	The college per-ceives little or no effect of the lib-rary's service and programs on student academic growth and development	1.962	4 (1.0%)	5.032	1.401

How successful is the library in achieving the following?
Please mark the appropriate response using the scale below.

Very Successful (7, 6) — Moderately Successful (5, 4, 3) — Unsuccessful (2, 1)

7 6 5 4 3 2 1

Item	V	M	ME	S.D.
_____59. Acquisition of materials to meet anticipated curricular needs of the college.	1.543	4 (1.0%)	4.971	1.242
_____60. Paying library staff salaries or wages commensurate with those paid to employees of comparable educational institutions.	2.873	6 (1.6%)	4.312	1.695
_____61. Accurately and completely accounting for all library materials at all times.	1.606	6 (1.6%)	4.934	1.267

Please rate the relative importance that <u>this library</u> places on each of the following factors. Please use the following scale for the rating.

Extremely Important — Not at all Important

7 6 5 4 3 2 1

Item	V	M	ME	S.D.
_____62. Librarian understanding of and support for the mission and goals of the college	1.408	----	5.792	1.187
_____63. Active involvement of the librarians in the total life of the college community	1.766	----	5.253	1.329
_____64. Responsiveness of the library to the requirements of the college's educational programs and curricula	1.104	1 (0.3%)	5.945	1.051
_____65. Student participation in the selection of library materials	1.800	----	2.583	1.342
_____66. Full-time faculty participation in the selection of library materials	1.960	3 (0.8%)	5.467	1.400

Extremely Important 7 6 5 4 3 2 1 Not at all Important	V	M	ME	S.D.
_____67. Membership and active participation in formal bibliographic and service cooperatives	1.935	3 (0.8%)	5.611	1.391
_____68. Participation of the librarians in the development of the library's annual budget recommendations	3.572	3 (0.8%)	4.507	1.890
_____69. Participation of the librarians in decisions regarding expenditures from the budget	2.929	1 (0.3%)	4.775	1.711
_____70. Maintaining formal or informal cooperative relationships with neighboring college libraries	1.971	----	5.451	1.404
_____71. Maintaining formal or informal cooperative relationships with neighboring high school libraries	3.026	1 (0.3%)	2.950	1.740
_____72. Maintaining formal or informal cooperative relationships with neighboring public libraries	2.951	1 (0.3%)	3.826	1.718
_____73. Evaluation of the collection by comparison with lists of key literature	2.584	4 (1.0%)	4.642	1.607
_____74. Evaluation of the collection by professional assessment by librarians	2.221	5 (1.3%)	4.963	1.490
_____75. Evaluation of the collection by judgement by qualified faculty	2.391	3 (0.8%)	4.633	1.546
_____76. Regular evaluation of its services and programs	2.506	3 (0.8%)	4.654	1.583
_____77. Development of innovative ways to perform its tasks and services	2.198	3 (0.8%)	5.042	1.483

Extremely Important						Not at all Important	V	M	ME	S.D.
7	6	5	4	3	2	1				

Item	V	M	ME	S.D.
_____78. Maintaining regular formal communication between library staff and library management	2.869	3 (0.8%)	5.223	1.694
_____79. Maintaining regular formal communications between library and its users	2.598	4 (1.0%)	4.582	1.612
_____80. Inclusion of librarians as members of the college's faculty (regardless of whether librarians have such membership or not)	2.814	2 (0.5%)	5.702	1.677
_____81. Wherever available, providing full MARC cataloging for library materials.	1.816	6 (1.6%)	6.159	1.347
_____82. Encouraging the development and use of a reserve collection.	1.854	3 (0.8%)	5.583	1.362

Please mark the appropriate response using the following scale:

7. All
6. A large majority
5. More than half
4. About half
3. Less that half
2. A small minority
1. None

Item	V	M	ME	S.D.
_____83. How many librarians have second master's degrees in disciplines represented by the College's curricula?	3.154	3 (0.8%)	3.451	1.776
_____84. How many librarians are trained in the use of computers for library management or services?	2.991	3 (0.8%)	5.029	1.730
_____85. How many full time faculty are involved in the selection of library materials?	3.124	9 (2.3%)	4.437	1.767

7. All
6. A large majority
5. More than half
4. About half
3. Less that half
2. A small minority
1. None

	V	M	ME	S.D.
____86. How many librarians participate in the selection of library materials?	2.901	6 (1.6%)	5.685	1.703
____87. How many librarians actively promote the spiritual, cultural and social life of this college?	3.280	7 (1.8%)	4.098	1.811
____88. How many library positions are covered by written job descriptions?	4.726	6 (1.6%)	5.545	2.174
____89. How many of the library's personnel recommendations affecting librarians are fully supported by the college adminis-tration	2.259	12 (3.1%)	5.288	1.503
____90. How many librarians hold membership in professional associations?	2.219	2 (0.5%)	5.691	1.490
____91. How many librarians are engaged in professional association activities?	2.965	2 (0.5%)	4.212	1.722
____92. How many librarians are involved in either formal or informal continuing education?	3.284	3 (0.8%)	3.974	1.812
____93. How many clerical staff are involved in either formal or informal continuing education?	1.992	3 (0.8%)	2.782	1.411
____94. How many staff members, in positions which this library considers professional, have masters degrees in library or information science from a school accredited by the ALA?	2.623	3 (0.8%)	6.157	1.619
____95. How many librarians are considered members of the college's faculty?	5.314	5 (1.3%)	5.517	2.305

Please place a check mark next to the <u>ONE</u> title below which most nearly describes your position title or responsibilities (even if you do other things, also).

_____ Director
_____ Professional Assistant to the Director
_____ Associate Director
_____ Assistant Director
_____ Head, Public Services
_____ Head, Technical Services
_____ Head, Cataloging
_____ Head, Reference
_____ Head, Library-Use Instruction
_____ Head, Branch or Campus Library

_____ Please send me a copy of the study's findings and conclusions

Appendix 3

QUESTIONNAIRE ITEMS KEYED TO EFFECTIVENESS CRITERIA

1	E 1	17	I 6
2	E 1	18	P 9
3	E 1	19	P 12
4	E 2	20	I 11
5	E 8	21	I 11
6	I 8	22	I 11
7	I 8	23	I 12
8	I 21	24	O 2
9	I 18	25	O 4
10	I 18	26	O 4
11	I 7	27	I 10
12	I 17	28	P 1
13	I 20	29	P 2
14	I 5	30	P 2
15	I 5	31	P 5
16	I 6	32	P 5

33	E 9	60	P 15
34	I 12	61	O 10
35	I 4	62	E 3
36	P 6	63	E 7
37	P 4	64	E 4
38	I 15	65	I 16
39	I 15	66	I 16
40	I 13	67	E 5
41	P 3	68	I 1
42	P 6	69	I 3
43	P 11	70	E 6
44	P 17	71	E 6
45	P 18	72	E 6
46	P 19	73	I 9
47	P 19	74	I 9
48	I 16	75	I 9
49	I 14	76	O 13
50	O 8	77	O 1
51	O 12	78	P 16
52	O 12	79	O 3
53	O 6	80	P 7
54	O 9	81	I 13
55	O 6	82	O 11
56	O 7	83	P 9
57	O 5	84	P 10
58	O 14	85	I 16
59	I 19	86	I 16

87	E 7	92	P 13
88	P 6	93	P 13
89	P 17	94	P 8
90	P 14	95	P 7
91	P 14		

Appendix 4

SAMPLE CHARACTERISTICS

Institutions	(N = 131)	
Affiliation	Federal:	3 (2.2%)
	State:	39 (29.8%)
	Private-Secular:	49 (37.5%)
	Private-Religious:	40 (30.5%)
Locations	Delaware:	2 (1.5%)
	Dist. of Columbia:	2 (1.5%)
	Maryland:	9 (6.9%)
	New Jersey:	13 (9.9%)
	New York:	45 (34.4%)
	Ohio:	27 (20.6%)
	Pennsylvania:	33 (25.2%)
Enrollments	Under 1,000:	29 (22.1%)
	1,000 - 1,999:	32 (24.4%)
	2,000 - 2,999:	17 (13.0%)
	3,000 - 3,999:	11 (8.4%)
	4,000 - 4,999:	12 (9.2%)
	5,000 - 5,999:	9 (6.9%)
	6,000 - 6,999:	8 (6.1%)
	Above 7,000:	13 (9.9%)

Libraries (N = 131)

Size of Collections:

Under 50,000:	11 (8.4%)
50,000 - 99,999:	20 (15.3%)
100,000 - 149,999:	16 (12.2%)
150,000 - 199,999:	23 (17.6%)
200,000 - 249,999:	18 (13.7%)
250,000 - 299,999:	10 (7.6%)
300,000 - 349,999:	6 (4.6%)
350,000 - 399,999:	8 (6.1%)
400,000 - 449,999:	5 (3.8%)
Over 500,000:	9 (6.9%)

Size of Staffs (N = 106); data not available for 25 libraries)

		Number of Professionals							
		0-2	3-5	6-8	9-11	12-14	15-17	18-20	20+
Number of Non-Professional/ Clerical	0-2	5.7*	3.8	1.9	-	-	-	-	-
	3-5	4.7	11.7	2.8	-	-	-	-	-
	6-8	0.9	7.5	8.5	0.9	-	-	-	-
	9-11	-	3.8	5.7	2.8	-	0.9	-	-
	12-14	-	0.9	4.7	2.8	1.9	-	-	-
	15-17	-	-	3.8	2.8	0.9	2.8	-	-
	18-20	-	-	1.9	0.9	0.9	-	0.9	0.9
	Over 20	-	-	-	1.9	3.8	2,8	-	3.8

*Numbers are percent of the sample with this combination of professional and non-professional/clerical staff.

Respondents* (N = 384)

Director:	118 (30.7%)
Professional Assistant to the Director:	7 (1.8%)
Associate Director:	16 (4.2%)
Assistant Director:	22 (5.7%)
Head, Public Services:	50 (13.0%)
Head, Technical Services:	45 (11.7%)
Head, Cataloging:	45 (11.7%)
Head, Reference:	50 (13.0%)
Head, Library-use Instr.	20 (5.2%)
Head, Branch or Campus Library	11 (2.9%)

*Respondents were asked to identify the one title from the list which most nearly described their position title or responsibilities.

Appendix 5

STATISTICAL ANALYSIS

The following sections contain a detailed and technical description of the statistical procedures employed in the analysis of the data collected in the 1986 academic library effectiveness study. For a more general and broadly based discussion of these matters, the reader is referred to Chapter 6.

INITIAL EXAMINATION OF DATA

The data were analyzed in several stages, using SPSS/PC+ and SPSSX statistical computer programs. At this point, the data had not been aggregated by institution.

The first step involved the derivation of descriptive statistics using the scores of each individual respondent. Each question (referred to hereafter as a variable) was examined for measures of dispersion and central tendency. Appendix Two contains the questionnaire with the variance, percent of missing responses, mean, and standard deviation for each question.

Table A.5–1 lists the questions with low variance (<1.0) or a high missing response rate (>4.0%). In only three instances was the variance found to be less than 1.0 (q50, q55, q57). The decision was made to retain these variables at this stage of analysis. One variable (q42), which had a missing response rate of 21.9 percent, was removed from further analysis. All other variables had a missing response rate of less than 4.0 percent and were retained. Procedures for handling missing responses varied with the statistical tests employed, and are discussed below.

The second step in the analysis was to generate a correlation matrix of all the remaining variables. The objective was to examine the data for multicolinearity and to remove variables which showed high intercorrelations (>.8000). Items showing correlations between .7000 and .8000 were also examined for possible elimination.

Table A.5–2 lists variables showing intercorrelations above .8000. Each instance

Table A.5–1
Questions with Low Variance or High Missing Response Rate

Question 50	The library provides sufficient indexing material to enable users to identify most of the material required regardless of its location on or off campus. Variance = .956
Question 55	Librarians provide informal guidance in the use of the library. Variance = .631
Question 57	Library staff provides prompt, courteous and reliable service. Variance = .758
Question 42	Written job descriptions are precise and complete. Missing Response = 21.9%

Table A.5–2
Variable Correlations >.8000

Variables	r^2	Action Taken
q9 to q10	(.8768)	q10 eliminated
q14 to q15	(.8768)	q15 eliminated
q14 to q16	(.8163)	q16 eliminated
q16 to q17	(.8805)	q17 eliminated
q15 to q17	(.8610)	both eliminated
q68 to q69	(.8119)	q69 eliminated

q9. The library annually acquires materials of sufficient breadth and depth to support the emphases of the college's curricula.

q10. The library annually acquires materials of sufficient currency to support the emphases of the college's curricula.

q14. Facilities are adequate for the library's tasks.

q15. Facilities are adequate for the library users' requirements.

q16. Furniture and equipment are sufficient to meet the library's task requirements.

q17. Furniture and equipment are sufficient to meet the library users' requirements.

q68. Librarians participate in the development of the library's annual budget.

q69. Librarians participate in decisions regarding expenditures from the library's annual budget.

Table A.5–3
Variable Correlations Between .7000 and .8000

Variables	r^2	Action Taken
q6 to q7	(.7936)	q7 eliminated
q9 to q12	(.7629)	q12 eliminated
q38 to q39	(.7693)	both retained
q48 to q65	(.7447)	q65 eliminated

q6. The existing collection is sufficient in breadth and depth to support the curricula.

q7. The existing collection is sufficient in currency to support the curricula.

q9. The library annually acquires materials of sufficient breadth to support the curricula.

q12. The library annually acquires materials of sufficient quantity to support the learning and teaching needs of its users.

q38. The library's collection development is well-planned and carefully monitored.

q39. The library's collections are developed in response to changes in the curriculum and patterns of use.

q48. Students are consistently involved in the selection of library materials.

q65. It is important that students participate in the selection of library materials.

above .8000 was reviewed individually, and a decision was made as to which variable to eliminate. The variable retained was the one which in the judgment of the researcher seemed to reflect best the intent of the criterion on which it was based. For example, question 9 correlated with question 10 at .8524. Both variables relate to the acquisition of library materials. One asks for information on the breadth and depth of annual acquisitions (q9), and the other seeks data on the currency of annual acquisitions (q10). It appeared to the researcher that respondents did not distinguish one from the other. Because breadth and depth probably implied currency, the decision was made to keep q9 and to drop q10.

Table A.5–3 lists variables showing intercorrelations between .7000 and .8000. In three of the cases, one variable was chosen to be deleted, using the method described above. In one instance (q38 and q39), the decision was made to retain both variables. This was done because it was felt that each question assessed a sufficiently different aspect of collection development, and because the correlation was below .8000. The relationship between these variables is explored in Chapter 6.

FACTOR ANALYSIS TO IDENTIFY DIMENSIONS

The remaining set of eighty-six variables were subjected to exploratory factor analysis in an attempt to discover underlying dimensions of library organizational-level effectiveness. The extraction method used was maximum likelihood with an oblique rotation. This followed Afifi and Clark's recommendation that when the

Table A.5–4
Variables with Communalities <.4000

Variable	Communality
q8	.39515
q82	.32151
q83	.38574
q84	.35453
q88	.32579
q94	.31602

q8. Materials purchased represent the variety of forms in which information is presented or distributed.

q82. It is important to encourage the development and use of a reserve collection.

q83. How many librarians have second master's degrees in disciplines represented by the college's curricula?

q84. How many librarians are trained in the use of computers for library management of services?

q88. How many library positions are covered by written job descriptions?

q94. How many staff members, in positions which this library considers professional, have masters degrees in library or information science from a school accredited by ALA?

researcher is satisfied that the factor model is valid and that the variables exhibit a normal distribution, the maximum likelihood (ML) method is preferred (Afifi and Clark, 1984).

The statistics for the initial factor analysis revealed a Kaiser-Meyer-Olkin measure of sampling adequacy of .87498. This suggested that the factor model is appropriate for these data. Kaiser (1974) indicates that measures in the .90s are "marvelous," measures in the .80s are "meritorious," measures in the .70s are "middling," measures in the .60s are "mediocre," measures in the .50s are "miserable," and measures below .50 are "unacceptable." Likewise, since Bartlett's test of sphericity showed a .0000 observed significance level, it could be assumed that the correlation matrix underlying the factor analysis is an identity matrix. Finally, the matrix of anti-image correlations revealed that only 1.1 percent of the off-diagonal elements are >0.09. These statistics further supported the use of a factor model for these data.

The oblique rotation was used because the data were known to be intercorrelated, and "an oblique rotation does not arbitrarily impose the restriction that factors be uncorrelated" (Kim and Mueller, 1978, p. 37). Cases with missing values were deleted listwise.

An examination of the initial statistics revealed six variables with communalities below .4000 (Table A.5–4). These were eliminated from further analysis. One

Table A.5–5
Variables Comprising Factor Twelve

Question 34	The approved budget is very close to the director's recommendations. Loading = (.58231)
Question 44	Evaluation by both peers and library administration is the basis for personnel recommendations affecting librarians. Loading = (.32424)
Question 87	How many librarians participate in the spiritual, cultural and social life of this college? Loading = (.30227)

additional variable, q35 (library director is solely responsible for expenditure of budget funds), was also eliminated. Its communality (.40914) was above the threshold for exclusion. However, it appeared to be measuring a trivial aspect of the budget issue better addressed in q34 (the approved budget is very close to the director's recommendations).

The remaining seventy-nine variables were re-factored again using the maximum likelihood method with an oblique rotation. A review of the loadings of the variables on their respective factors revealed that only one, q43 (the library provides the staff with opportunities to receive required training), loaded below a .3000. Because it explained only .8 percent of the variance, this variable was also removed. Those remaining were again re-factored using maximum likelihood extraction and oblique rotation.

The resulting pattern matrix can be found in the original report of this work (McDonald, 1987). It reveals twenty-one factors with eigenvalues >1.0. The associated statistics show a Kaiser-Meyer-Olkin measure of sampling adequacy of .86119. As before, Bartlett's test of sphericity showed a .0000 observed significance level. The matrix of anti-image correlations showed 1.5 percent of the off-diagonals to be >0.09.

At this point, the factors were examined for interpretability. Twenty of the twenty-one factors were interpretable. Six of these were improved by the elimination of one variable each. In all cases, the variable removed had the lowest loading on its factor. These variables, as well as the uninterpretable factor, Factor Twelve (Table A.5–5), were removed from further data analysis.

The twenty interpretable factors were separated into two groups. Factors with two variables were designated as "minor" factors, while those with three or more variables were designated "major" ones. This follows Thurstone's suggestion (1947) that there be at least three variables for each factor in exploratory analysis.

DIMENSIONS OF EFFECTIVENESS

A complete list of the variables comprising each of the major and minor factors appears in Appendix 6. Because these factors would seem to be an adequate representation of the grouping of elements of effectiveness as revealed by the data, they are hereafter referred to as "dimensions."

Although a total of twenty-one dimensions were identified, the decision was taken to continue the investigation using only the thirteen major ones. This decision was made after the dimensions themselves were factored in an attempt to group similar dimensions and thus to further reduce the number of variables required to "explain" the data. When the minor dimensions were included in the second-order factoring, the resulting factors were uninterpretable. Removing them, however, made the factors of the dimensions interpretable. This factoring of the dimensions (to create "domains") is discussed further, below.

At this point, the raw data were aggregated to produce mean institutional scores for each of the 131 libraries for each of the variables. Following this, institutional scores for each of the dimensions were computed by averaging the library's scores for the appropriate variables. The dimensions were then tested for discriminant validity and reliability, using the dimension scores. The correlation matrix for the dimensions can be found in McDonald (1987). The correlation matrix for the dimensions showed that some of them are moderately related, but the overall impression is that the dimensions are distinct. Also available (McDonald, 1987) are the reliability coefficients for each of the thirteen major dimensions. Only two of the dimensions show reliability coefficients below .7000. This suggests that the dimensions are composed of items with high internal consistency.

In order to test the discriminant validity of the dimensions, the average within-dimension correlation (intra-scale correlation) for each variable was compared to its average correlation with all variables outside its own effectiveness dimension (inter-scale correlation). The results of this analysis (McDonald, 1987) revealed that the average intra-dimension correlation was higher than the average inter-dimension correlation for all but six of the fifty-five variables. This confirms that the dimensions are composed of items which distinguish one dimension from another.

FACTOR ANALYSIS TO IDENTIFY DOMAINS

The next step in the data analysis involved factoring the major dimensions. This second-order factoring was undertaken in an attempt to identify the smallest number of variables associated with library effectiveness. Such a reduction in the number of variables, if possible, would also allow the third research question to be answered. This question asks whether it is possible to identify groups of academic libraries which show high effectiveness in contrast with others which show lower effectiveness. Because of the large number of cases (institutions) in this study, it was thought that it would be more manageable to cluster against a few "domains" than against thirteen dimensions.

The results of the factor analysis are shown in McDonald, 1987. A full list of variables composing each domain is given in Appendix 7.

CLUSTER ANALYSIS

Clustering techniques can be classed, broadly, into nonhierarchical and hierarchical methods. Many reasons can be advanced for choosing one method or the other. Lorr (1983), however, notes the reasons for selecting hierarchical methods. First, he points to the poor performance obtained when using nonhierarchical methods without good starting points, a common problem. On the positive side, he indicates that criteria have been developed for finding the level in a hierarchy at which there is an optimum number of clusters. Finally, a hierarchical method is required whenever developmental arrangement of the clusters is sought (the usual case).

Hierarchical clustering methods can be classed as agglomerative or divisive. Agglomerative methods, the most popular of the clustering techniques (Lorr, 1983, p. 84), begin with each entity to be clustered considered as a separate cluster. The selected algorithm is then used to combine the entities into successively larger clusters until only one cluster remains.

The agglomerative hierarchical methods divide into three basic approaches: linkage methods, centroid methods, and minimum-variance methods. The linkage methods further divide into single linkage, complete linkage, and average linkage. In average linkage, the method chosen for clustering the libraries in this study, "each member of a cluster has a smaller average disimilarity with other members of the same cluster than with members of any other cluster" (Lorr, 1983, p. 88). Norusis (1986, p. B-83) further explains that average linkage

> defines the distance between two clusters as the average of the distances between all pairs of cases in which one member of the pair is from each of the clusters. For example, if cases 1 and 2 form Cluster A and cases 3, 4, and 5 form Cluster B, the distance between Cluster A and B is taken to be the average of the distances between the following pairs of cases: (1,3) (1,4) (1,5) (2,3) (2,4) (2,5). This differs from the linkage methods in that it uses information about all pairs of distances, not just the nearest or the furtherest. For this reason, it is usually preferred to the single and complete linkage methods of cluster analysis.

Norusis also states that average linkage can be used with either similarity or distance measures, implying that squared Euclidean distances (the distance measure chosen for this study) is appropriate.

Another issue to be determined in cluster analysis is the choice of the number of clusters. In both agglomerative and divisive methods, the researcher may chose between one cluster (all cases) and N clusters (the n of the cases). For this research, the agglomeration schedule produced by SPSS PC+ was used to determine the number of clusters.

Finally, Lorr (1983, pp. 104–121) addresses the question of which algorithms are the most effective in recovering an underlying structure. He discusses the results of more than thirty empirical studies of the cluster methods, including a number of recent Monte Carlo validation studies. He observes that the problem of cluster recovery is complex, but that recent Monte Carlo evaluative studies strongly suggest that the group-average linkage method is the most accurate of the hierarchical techniques.

Accordingly, in this research, the cluster method chosen was the group-average linkage with squared Euclidean distances, and the computer-generated agglomeration schedule, exhibiting five clearly distinguishable clusters, was used as the "stopping rule." The results of the cluster analysis are presented and discussed in Chapter 7.

PROBLEM OF CONSTRUCT VALIDITY

Validity, generally, can be defined as the extent to which a measuring instrument measures what it is supposed to be measuring. The three most basic types of validity typically and traditionally used in the social sciences are criterion, content, and construct validity. However, Schneider and Schmitt (1986) observe that recently there has been recognition that the distinctions among them are artificial. They note that all validation work is really an aspect of construct validity. Accordingly, below, we will focus on construct validity and refer the reader to McDonald (1987) for a thorough discussion of the relationship among criterion, content, and construct validity as it affects the validity of this study.

Construct validity "is defined as representing the correspondence between a construct (conceptual definition of a variable) and the operational procedure used to measure or manipulate that construct" (Schwab, 1986, p. 5). In other words, does the measure really measure what it purports to be measuring? Construct validity also represents the degree to which test scores are consistent with theory about what the test measures. Price and Mueller (1986) note that assessing this latter relationship involves defining the theoretical relationship, obtaining the empirical relationship, and then comparing the two. The empirical verification of the hypothesized relationship is then used to support the construct validity of the measure.

There are four basic problems encountered in any attempt to establish construct validity. First, there are no standards for deciding the magnitude of the empirical relationship needed to claim validity. Second, there are interpretation difficulties when the empirical relationship does not match the theory. The theory may be incorrect, the procedure to check the relationship may be incorrect, the invalidity may rest in the measure of the other concept(s) in the relationship, or, the measure may, in fact, genuinely lack construct validity. The latter is usually inferred, but there are three other possibilities for the measure-theory mismatch.

Third, the theory frequently is incomplete and does not clearly specify whether the relationship being checked is zero-order or a partial relationship net of other variables. Most assessments of construct validity involve zero-order relationships. However, theories tend to be multivariate, and construct validity should be assessed with regard to net relationships.

Finally, most theories involving organizations are in such an early stage of development that it is difficult if not impossible to hypothesize the strength of relationships among variables. This makes the assessment of construct validity considerably less than precise.

The fundamental problem in assessing the validity of the effectiveness construct in this study is the absence of theory and the inability to fit the results of the investigation into a network of expected relationships among library effectiveness variables. This study breaks new ground and its findings—that effectiveness is a multivariate, multidimensional construct and varies with the domains in which a library has determined it needs to function—provide evidence for a phenomenon that does not appear, heretofore, to have been adduced in research on the organizational effectiveness of academic libraries.

This study has begun to contribute to empirically defensible theory- building on library effectiveness. But such theory cannot be advanced successfully until there is some confidence that the construct presumably measured here does, in fact, exist "in reality." If perceptual data of this study, by themselves, cannot be used to demonstrate construct validity, there are two approaches to further research which may contribute to such validity.

In the first approach, confirmatory factor analysis may be able to provide evidence of validity of sufficient strength to warrant some confidence in the construct. Kerlinger (1973) points out that factor analysis is perhaps the most powerful method of construct validation available. To study the construct validity of any measure it is helpful to correlate the measure with other measures. And it is certainly more valuable to correlate a measure with a large number of other measures. One of the best ways to learn about a construct is to know its correlates, and factor analysis is a refined method of doing this. It tells us, in effect, what measures measure the same thing and to what extent they measure what they measure.

The present study has identified a number of effectiveness dimensions as perceived by library decision makers. If subsequent research can confirm (through factor analysis) that these dimensions also exist in other library samples (as perceived by the dominant coalition), it would appear that the validity of the questionnaire test measures could be demonstrated and then strengthened by even further research.

A second approach to the validity of the effectiveness measures is to use the multitrait-multimethod matrix method described by Campbell and Fiske (1959). According to Schneider and Schmitt (1986), underlying the use of the multitrait-multimethod matrix is the idea that a measure of some phenomena should correlate highly with other measures of the same phenomena *and* that it should not correlate with measures of different phenomena from which it should theoretically differ. They point out that when a measure of a phenomenon correlates highly with other measures of the same phenomenon, this indicates convergent validity. When the test does not correlate with measures of other phenomena, this indicates discriminant validity.

Without valid alternative measures of the construct, however, it is impossible to demonstrate convergent or discriminant validity. And, recently, it has been recognized that the multitrait-multimethod provides only limited evidence about construct validity (Schwab, 1986) because if convergence is to demonstrate validity, the methods used must be assumed to be uncorrelated. It is usually difficult to show that convergent variance does not reflect method variance. It is likely, then, that convergence is not much better than reliability as a test of construct validity.

Cameron (1978b) attempted to demonstrate convergent and discriminant validity through multitrait-multimethod matrices. In essence, he argued that the convergence of the scores of the various classes of respondents on the various dimensions was sufficient to suggest some validity. Furthermore, an examination of the matrices' correlations suggested evidence of discriminant validity. Although this is a creative use of the multitrait-multimethod approach, its use in this way seems questionable. The phenomenon under investigation—organizational-level effectiveness—was measured by all respondents using the same method. A true convergence of methods was not demonstrated, nor was a lack of correlation shown with measures of different phenomena from which effectiveness should, in theory, differ.

In summary, the research reported here has used a test instrument (a questionnaire) to measure a phenomenon called effectiveness. The validity of this measurement will rest, ultimately, in evidence collected from a variety of sources, in a variety of ways, over time. As Selltiz, Jahoda, Deutsch, and Cook (1959) point out, construct validity cannot be adequately tested by any single procedure. How evidence from different sources bears on estimation of the validity of the original measurement depends on the relationships predicted in the theoretical structure of the construct. The more different relationships tested and confirmed, the greater the support, for both the measuring instrument and the underlying theory.

Accordingly, it would seem that the development of library organizational-level effectiveness theory is a fundamental precursor to efforts to validate test measures of the construct. As with many other constructs in the social sciences, theory is established and advanced by measurement efforts such as those reported here.

Appendix 6

VARIABLES COMPRISING MAJOR AND MINOR FACTORS

MAJOR FACTORS

Factor Three: Library Collection Adequacy

q6 existing collection contains materials of sufficient breadth and depth to support the curricula. (.86367)

q11 size of collection is large enough to meet user needs (.81642)

q9 the library acquires materials of sufficient breadth and depth to support the curricula (.67907)

q13 the library acquires materials to support faculty research (.50408)

q27 library users are able to secure needed materials from the collection (.47765)

q59 the library acquires materials to meet anticipated curricular needs (.46692)

q1 the annual budget is adequate (.35624)

Factor Four: Bibliographic Access/Use of Library's Collections

q25 students make regular use of library materials and services (.94050)

q26 faculty make regular use of library materials and services (.55193)

q49 the library's cataloging system is easily understood and used by faculty and students (.25524)

Factor Five: Bibliographic Access/Use of Extramural Library Collections

q51 the library maintains a formal and well-publicized interlibrary loan service (.84728)

q52 users are able to obtain promptly materials not owned by the library (.65091)

q67 active participation in formal bibliographic cooperatives is important to the library (.33818)

q54 machine-readable bibliographic database searching is easily obtained through the library (.30445)

q50 the library provides sufficient indexing material to enable users to identify most of the material required regardless of its location on or off campus (.26039)

Factor Six: Library/Users' Shared Goals

q28 library goals are explicitly stated (.78046)

q29 library goals are agreed upon by library management and librarians (.75251)

q30 efforts are made to secure input from users in the development of library goals (.47869)

q24 the library publicizes its services so that users know they exist (.37520)

Factor Seven: Staff Development

q92 librarians are involved in formal or informal continuing education (.94610)

q93 clerical staff are involved in formal or informal continuing education (.57225)

q91 librarians are engaged in professional association activities (.39014)

q90 librarians hold membership in professional associations (.32610)

Factor Eight: Staff Size and Diversity

q2 the professional staff is adequate (.86535)

q31 the library staff is large enough to accomplish the library's work (.71630)

q3 the clerical staff is adequate (.56141)

q32 the library staff has people with a sufficient diversity of skills (.48641)

q53 a librarian is always available to help users (.21986)

Factor Nine: Librarian/Faculty Relations

q80 the library considers it important that librarians are members of faculty (.69970)

q95 librarians in this library are members of college faculty (.69464)

q33 librarians and teaching faculty interact as professional colleagues in the pursuit of the college's academic objectives (.48366)

q63 librarians are actively involved in the total life of the college (.35955)

q81* the library considers it important that full MARC cataloging be provided (.29767)

Factor Ten: Evaluation of Library

q74 the library considers it important that the collection be evaluated by librarians (.81152)

q75 the library considers it important that the collection be evaluated by qualified faculty (.62623)

q73 the library considers it important that its collections be evaluated by comparison with lists of key literature (.60255)

q76 the library considers it important that its services and programs be regularly evaluated (.34752)

Factor Thirteen: Cooperative Associations

q71 maintaining cooperative relationships with high school libraries is important to the library (.74623)

q72 maintaining cooperative relationships with neighboring public libraries is important to the library (.74068)

q70 maintaining cooperative relationships with neighboring college libraries is important to the library (.37815)

Factor Fourteen: College Support for Library

q5 faculty support for library programs and services is adequate (.61264)

q4 college support for library innovation is adequate (.53479) q58 the college perceives the library as having a positive effect on student academic growth (.46473)

q48* students are involved in the selection of library materials (.30114)

Factor Sixteen: Shared Organizational Direction

q78 the library considers it important to maintain formal communication between library staff and management (.61347)

q68 the library considers it important that librarians participate in budget recommendations (.47129)

q41 library policies and decisions are the joint responsibility of librarians and library administration (.46054)

q79 the library considers it important to maintain formal communication between the library and its users (.34566)

q77 the library considers it important to develop innovative ways to perform its tasks and services (.32968)

q86 librarians participate in the selection of library materials (.31865)

Factor Seventeen: Librarian Professional Service

q55 librarians provide informal guidance in the use of the library (.63750)

q56 librarians are involved in formal efforts to teach information-seeking skills (.57796)

q57 library staff provides prompt, courteous, and reliable service (.49820)

q36 librarians are skilled in the application of professional knowledge to the solution of specific problems and the attainment of goals and objectives (.35602)

Factor Nineteen: Collections' Physical Organization

q23 most heavily used materials are shelved in the most accessible locations (.53727)

q22 materials are organized so that they are readily accessible (.53023) q21 space for shelving and storage is efficiently used (.39042)

q18* librarians are appointed to positions that match their education and experience with their responsibilities (.33747)

MINOR FACTORS

Factor One: Staff Morale

q46 clerical staff exhibit a positive and optimistic spirit (1.04067)

q47 librarians exhibit a positive and optimistic spirit (.52470)

Factor Two: Collection Development

q38: the library's collection development is well planned and monitored (.93346)

q39 the library makes a strong effort to develop its collections in response to changes in the curriculum (.69541)

Factor Eleven: Facilities

q14 facilities are adequate for the library's tasks (.78428)

q20 sufficient space is provided to shelve all of the library's collections (.77448)

Factor Fifteen: Library Perception of College Needs

q64 the library considers it important that it be responsive to the requirements of the college's curricula (.62504)

q62 the library considers it important that librarians understand and support the mission and goals of the college (.58680)

q89* the library's personnel recommendations affecting librarians are fully supported by college administration (.25508)

Factor Eighteen: Management Technique

q19 the library provides appropriate opportunities and rewards for professional development (.51266)

q37 organizational management techniques are consciously used in the administration of the library (.33910)

q45* clerical staff are regularly evaluated by their immediate supervisors (.26177)

Factor Twenty: Materials Control

q61 the library is very successful at accurately accounting for all library materials at all times (.56154) q40 the catalog accurately represents the contents of the library's collections (.25671)

Factor Twenty-One: Faculty Involvement in Materials Selection

q85 all full-time faculty are involved in the selection of library materials (.47482)

q66 the library considers it important that full-time faculty participate in the selection of library materials (.45294)

q60* the library is able to pay library staff salaries commensurate with those paid to employees of comparable educational institutions (.38569)

Appendix 7

DOMAINS: THEIR DIMENSIONS AND VARIABLES

Numbers in parentheses are the loadings of the variables on the dimensions or the dimensions on the domains.

DOMAIN ONE: MAJOR RESOURCES

Dimension Three: Library Collection Adequacy (.98616)

q6 the existing collection contains materials of sufficient breadth and depth to support the curricula (.86367)

q11 the size of the collection is large enough to meet user needs (.81642)

q9 the library acquires materials of sufficient breadth and depth to support the curricula (.67907)

q13 the library acquires materials to support faculty research (.50408)

q27 library users are able to secure needed materials from the collection (.47765)

q59 the library acquires materials to meet anticipated curricular needs (.46692)

q1 the annual budget is adequate (.35624)

Dimension Eight: Staff Size and Diversity (.43188)

q2 the professional staff is adequate (.86535)

q31 the library staff is large enough to accomplish the library's work (.71630) q3 the clerical staff is adequate (.56141)

q32 the library staff has people with a sufficient diversity of skills (.48641)

q53 a librarian is always available to help users (.21986)

Dimension Fourteen: College Support for Library (.45877)

q5 faculty support for library programs and services is adequate (.61264)

q4 college support for library innovation is adequate (.53479)

q58 the college perceives the library as having a positive effect on student academic growth (.46473)

q48* students are involved in the selection of library materials (.30114)

DOMAIN TWO: SERVICES

Dimension Five: Bibliographic Access/Use of Extramural Library Collections (.96621)

q51 the library maintains a formal and well-publicized interlibrary loan service (.84728)

q52 users are able to obtain promptly materials not owned by the library (.65091)

q67 active participation in formal bibliographic cooperatives is important to the library (.33818)

q54 machine-readable bibliographic database searching is easily obtained through the library (.30445)

q50 the library provides sufficient indexing material to enable users to identify most of the material required regardless of its location on or off campus (.26039)

Dimension Thirteen: Cooperative Associations (.31980)

q71 maintaining cooperative relationships with high school libraries is important to the library (.74623)

q72 maintaining cooperative relationships with neighboring public libraries is important to the library (.74068)

q70 maintaining cooperative relationships with neighboring college libraries is important to the library (.37815)

Dimension Seventeen: Librarian Professional Service (.53870)

q55 librarians provide informal guidance in the use of the library (.63750)

q56 librarians are involved in formal efforts to teach information-seeking skills (.57796) q57 library staff provides prompt, courteous, and reliable service (.49820)

q36 librarians are skilled in the application of professional knowledge to the solution of specific problems and the attainment of goals and objectives (.35602)

DOMAIN THREE: LIBRARY/STAKEHOLDER INTERACTION

Dimension Six: Library/Users' Shared Goals (.62504)

q28 library goals are explicitly stated (.78046)

q29 library goals are agreed upon by library management and librarians (.75251)

q30 efforts are made to secure input from users in the development of library goals (.47869)

q24 the library publicizes its services so that users know they exist (.37520)

Dimension Seven: Staff Development (.27782)

q92 librarians are involved in formal or informal continuing education (.94610)

q93 clerical staff are involved in formal or informal continuing education (.57225)

q91 librarians are engaged in professional association activities (.39014)

q90 librarians hold membership in professional associations (.32610)

Dimension Nine: Librarian/Faculty Relations (.34119)

q80 the library considers it important that librarians are members of faculty (.69970)

q95 librarians in this library are members of college faculty (.69464)

q33 librarians and teaching faculty interact as professional colleagues in the pursuit of the college's academic objectives (.48366) q63 librarians are actively involved in the total life of the college (.35955)

q81* the library considers it important that full MARC cataloging be provided (.29767)

Dimension Ten: Evaluation of Library (.66100)

q74 the library considers it important that the collection be evaluated by librarians (.81152)

q75 the library considers it important that the collection be evaluated by qualified faculty (.62623)

q73 the library considers it important that the collection be evaluated by comparison with lists of key literature (.60255)

q76 the library considers it important to regularly evaluate its services and programs (.34752)

Dimension Sixteen: Shared Organizational Direction (.76417)

q78 the library considers it important to maintain formal communication between library staff and management (.61347)

q68 the library considers it important that librarians participate in budget recommendations (.47129)

q41 library policies and decisions are the joint responsibility of librarians and library administration (.46054)

q79 the library considers it important to maintain formal communication between the library and its users (.34566)

q79 the library considers it important to develop innovative ways to perform its tasks and services (.32968)

q86 librarians participate in the selection of library materials (.31865)

DOMAIN FOUR: ACCESS

Dimension Four: Bibliographic Access/Use of Library's Collections (.86610)

q25 students make regular use of library materials and services (.94050)

q26 faculty make regular use of library materials and services (.55193)

q49 the library's cataloging system is easily understood and used by faculty and students (.25524)

Dimension Nineteen: Collections' Physical Organization (.58632)

q23 most heavily used materials are shelved in the most accessible locations (.53727)

q22 materials are organized so that they are readily accessible (.53023)

q21 space for shelving and storage is efficiently used (.39042)

q18* librarians are appointed to positions that match their education and experience with their responsibilities (.33747)

BIBLIOGRAPHY

Abraham, Terry. 1980. "Managerial Rating: A Library Effectiveness Model." In *Library Effectiveness: A State of the Art*. Papers from a 1980 American Library Association Preconference. Chicago: American Library Association.

Afifi, A. A., and Virginia Clark. 1984. *Computer-Aided Multivariate Analysis*. Belmont, Calif.: Lifetime Learning Publications.

Allen, Kenneth S. 1972. *Current and Emerging Techniques in Academic Libraries, Including a Critique of the Model Budget Analysis Program of the State of Washington*. Washington, D.C.: Council on Library Resources.

Altman, E., E. R. DeProspo, P. M. Clark, and E. C. Clark. 1976. *A Data Gathering and Instructional Manual for Performance Measures in Public Libraries*. Chicago: Celdon Press.

American Library Association (ALA). 1958. *Catalogue Use Study*, ed. V. Mostecky. Chicago: ALA.

———. 1980. *Library Effectiveness: A State of the Art*. Chicago: ALA.

Argyris, Chris. 1962. *Interpersonal Competence and Organizational Effectiveness*. Homewood, Ill.: Irwin.

———. 1970. *Intervention Theory and Method: A Behavioral Science View*. Reading, Mass.: Addison-Wesley.

Baker, Sharon L., and F. Wilfrid Lancaster. 1991. *The Measurement and Evaluation of Library Services*. 2nd ed. Arlington, Va.: Information Resources Press.

Barney, J. 1977. *The Electronic Revolution in the Watch Industry*. New Haven, Conn.: School of Organization and Management, Yale University.

Bass, B. M. 1952. "Ultimate Criteria of Organizational Worth." *Personnel Psychology* 5:157–173.

Battin, Patricia. 1984. "The Library: Center of the Restructured University." *College and Research Libraries* 45 (May): 170–176.

Beasley, K. 1968. "A Theoretic Framework for Public Library Measurement." In *Research Methods in Librarianship: Measurement and Evaluation*, ed. H. Goldhor. Champaign, Ill.: University of Illinois Graduate School of Library Science.

Beaubien, Anne K., Sharon A. Hogan, and Mary W. George. 1982. *Learning the Library: Concepts and Methods for Effective Bibliographic Instruction*. New York: R. R. Bowker.

Beckhard, Richard. 1969. *Organizational Development*. Reading, Mass.: Addison-Wesley.

Bedeian, Arthur G. 1986. ''Contemporary Challenges in the Study of Organizations.'' *Journal of Management* 12:185–201.

Bennis, Warren G. 1966. ''The Concept of Organizational Health.'' In *Changing Organizations*, ed. Warren G. Bennis. New York: McGraw-Hill.

Bidwell, Charles E., and John O. Kasarda. 1975. ''School District Organization and Student Achievement.'' *American Sociological Review* 40:55–70.

Blau, Peter M., and W. Richard Scott. 1961. *Formal Organizations*. San Francisco: Chandler.

Boaz, M. 1968. ''Evaluation of Special Library Service for Upper Management.'' *Special Libraries* 59:789–791.

Bommer, Michael R. W., and Ronald W. Chorba. 1982. *Decision Making for Library Management*. White Plains, N.Y.: Knowledge Industry Publications.

Branscomb, Harvie. 1940. *Teaching with Books: A Study of College Libraries*. Chicago: Association of American Colleges and American Library Association.

Breivik, Patricia Senn, and E. Gordon Gee. 1989. *Information Literacy: Revolution in the Library*. New York: Macmillan.

Brooks, B., and F. G. Kilgour. 1964. ''Catalog Subject Searches in the Yale Medical Library.'' *College and Research Libraries* 25:483–487.

Brophy, Peter, G. Ford, A. Hindle, and A. G. MacKenzie. 1972. *The Library Management Game: A Report on a Research Project*. Lancaster, England: University of Lancaster.

Brophy, Peter, M. K. Buckland, and A. Hindle, eds. 1976. *Reader in Operations Research for Libraries*. Englewood, Colo.: Information Handling Services.

Brown, Donald R., Shirley M. Smith, and Robert A. Scott. 1984. ''Evaluating the Effectiveness of Academic Libraries and Computing Facilities.'' *Determining the Effectiveness of Campus Services*. New Directions for Institutional Research No. 40. San Francisco: Jossey-Bass.

Buckland, Michael K. 1975. *Book Availability and the Library User*. New York: Pergamon Press.

———. 1978. ''Ten Years' Progress in Quantitative Research on Libraries.'' *Socioeconomic Planning Sciences* 12:333–339.

———. 1983. *Library Services in Theory and Context*. New York: Pergamon Press.

Buzzard, M. L., and D. E. New. 1983. ''An Investigation of Collection Support for Doctoral Research.'' *College and Research Libraries* 44:469–475.

Cameron, Kim S. 1978a. ''Measuring Organizational Effectiveness in Institutions of Higher Education.'' *Administrative Science Quarterly* 2:604–629.

———. 1978b. ''Organizational Effectiveness: Its Measurement and Prediction in Higher Education.'' Ph.D. diss., Yale University.

———. 1980. ''Critical Questions in Assessing Organizational Effectiveness.'' *Organizational Dynamics* 9:66–80.

———. 1981. ''Construct Space and Subjectivity Problems in Organizational Effectiveness.'' *Public Productivity Review* 5 (June):105–121.

———. 1982. *Organizational Effectiveness: A Bibliography through 1981*. Boulder, Colo.: National Center for Higher Education Management Statistics.

———. 1986. "Effectiveness as Paradox: Consensus and Conflict in Conceptions of Organizational Effectiveness." *Management Science* 32:539–553.

Cameron, Kim S., and Mary Tschirhart. 1992. "Postindustrial Environments and Organizational Effectiveness in Colleges and Universities." *Journal of Higher Education* 63 (January-February): 87–108.

Cameron, Kim S., and David A. Whetten. 1981. "Perceptions of Organizational Effectiveness over Organizational Life Cycles." *Administrative Science Quarterly* 26:525–544.

———, eds. 1983. *Organizational Effectiveness: A Comparison of Multiple Models*. Orlando, Fla.: Academic Press.

Cameron, Kim S., Myung U. Kim, and David A. Whetten. 1987. "Organizational Effects of Decline and Turbulence." *Administrative Science Quarterly* 32:222–240.

Campbell, D. T., and D. W. Fiske. 1959. "Convergent and Discriminant Validation by the Multitrait-Multimethod Matrix." *Psychological Bulletin* 56:81–105.

Campbell, J. P. 1974. "Sources of Organizational Indicators." In *Proceedings from the Symposium on the Utilization of Indicator Data*. Ann Arbor: Institute for Social Research, University of Michigan.

Campbell, John P. 1977. "On the Nature of Organizational Effectiveness." In *New Perspectives on Organizational Effectiveness*, 13–53. *See* Goodman and Pennings, 1977.

Caplow, T. 1964. *Principles of Organization*. New York: Harcourt Brace Jovanovich.

Carlson, William Hugh. 1946. *College and University Libraries and Librarianship*. Chicago: ALA.

Carmines, Edward G., and Richard A. Zeller. 1979. *Reliability and Validity Assessment*. Beverly Hills: Sage.

Carnovsky, L. 1955. "Public Library Surveys and Evaluations." *Library Quarterly* 25:23–26.

———. 1959. "Evaluation and Library Services." *UNESCO Bulletin for Libraries* 13:221–225.

Chen, Ching-chih. 1976. *Applications of Operations Research Models to Libraries: A Case Study of the Use of Monographs in the Francis A. Countway Library of Medicine, Harvard University*. Cambridge, Mass.: MIT Press.

Cheng, Joseph L. C. 1984. "Organizational Coordination, Uncertainty, and Performance: An Integrative Study." *Human Relations* 37:829–851.

Cheng, Joseph L. C., and William McKinley. 1983. "Toward an Integration of Organization Research and Practice: A Contingency Study of Bureaucratic Control and Performance in Scientific Settings." *Administrative Science Quarterly* 28:85–100.

Child, J. 1974a. "Managerial and Organizational Factors Associated with Performance—Part 1." *Journal of Management Studies* 11:175–189.

———. 1974b. "What Determines Organizational Performance? The Universals vs. the It-all-depends." *Organizational Dynamics* (Summer):2–18.

———. 1975. "Managerial and Organizational Factors Associated with Company Performance—Part 2." *Journal of Management Studies* 12:12–27.

Childers, Thomas B., and Nancy Van House. 1989. "The Grail of Goodness: The Effective Public Library." *Library Journal* 114:44–49.

Clapp, V. W., and R. T. Jordan. 1965. "Quantitative Criteria for Adequacy of Academic Library Collections." *College and Research Libraries* 26:371–380.

Clark, B. R. 1970. *The Distinctive College*. Chicago: Aldine.

Clark, J. V. 1962. "A Healthy Organization." *California Management Review* 4:16–30.

Cummings, L. L. 1977. "Emergence of the Instrumental Organization." In *New Perspectives on Organizational Effectiveness*, 56–62. *See* Goodman and Pennings, 1977.

———. 1982. "Organizational Behavior." *Annual Review of Psychology* 33:563–564.

Damanpour, Fariborz, and William Evan. 1984. "Organizational Innovation and Performance: The Problem of 'Organizational Lag.' " *Administrative Science Quarterly* 29:392–408.

Davis, Hiram Logan. 1984. *An Analysis of the Relationship Between Actual and Preferred Library Goals Based on the Perceptions of Academic Librarians*. Ann Arbor: University of Michigan.

DePew, John N. 1983. "The ACRL Standards for Faculty Status: Panacea or Placebo?" *College and Research Libraries* 44:407.

DeProspo, Ernest R., and Ellen Altman. 1972. "Another Attempt at Measuring Public Library Effectiveness: Some Methodological Considerations." In *Approaches to Measuring Library Effectiveness: A Symposium. See* Hershfield and Boone, 1972.

"Descriptions of 101 Successful Uses of Computer Technology in College Classrooms." 1991. *Chronicle of Higher Education* 38 (October 16): A26–A38.

Dornbusch, Sanford M., and William R. Scott. 1975. *Evaluation and the Exercise of Authority*. San Francisco: Jossey-Bass.

Dougherty, R. 1972. "The Human Side of Library Effectiveness." In *Approaches to Measuring Library Effectiveness: A Symposium. See* Hershfield and Boone, 1972.

Dougherty, Richard M. 1991. "Point of View: Research Libraries Must Abandon the Idea That 'Bigger is Better.' " *Chronicle of Higher Education* 37 (June 19):A32.

Dougherty, Richard M., and Carol Hughes. 1991. *Preferred Futures for Libraries: A Summary of Six Workshops with University Provosts and Library Directors*. Mountain View, Calif.: Research Libraries Group.

Dubin, R. 1976. "Organizational Effectiveness: Some Dilemmas of Perspective." *Organization and Administrative Sciences* 7:7–14.

Du Mont, Rosemary Ruhig. 1980. "A Conceptual Basis for Library Effectiveness." *College and Research Libraries* 41:103–111.

Du Mont, Rosemary, and Paul F. Du Mont. 1979. "Measuring Library Effectiveness: A Review and Assessment." *Advances in Librarianship* 9:103–141.

Duncan, R. B. 1973. "Multiple Decision-making Structure in Adapting to Environmental Uncertainty: The Impact on Organizational Effectiveness." *Human Relations* 26:273–291.

Edwards, Richard L., Sue R. Faerman, and Michael R. McGrath. 1986. "The Competing Values Approach to Organizational Effectiveness." *Administration in Social Work* 10:1–14.

English, Thomas G. 1984. "Administrators' View of Library Personnel Status." *College and Research Libraries* 45:191–192.

Ettelt, H. J. 1978. "Book Use at a Small (Very) Community College Library." *Library Journal* 103:2314–2315.

Etzioni, Amitai. 1964. *Modern Organizations*. Englewood Cliffs, N.J.: Prentice-Hall.

Euster, Joanne R. 1986. "The Activities and Effectiveness of the Academic Library Director in the Environmental Context." Ph.D. diss., University of California, Berkeley.

Evans, Edward, Harold Borko, and Patricia Ferguson. 1972. "Review of Criteria Used to Measure Library Effectiveness." *Bulletin of the Medical Library Association* 60 (January):102–110.

Fact Book on Higher Education, 1986–87. 1987. New York: Macmillan.

Farber, Evan Ira, ed. 1991. *Teaching and Technology: The Impact of Unlimited Information Access on Classroom Teaching: Proceedings of a National Forum at Earlham College*. Ann Arbor, Mich.: Pierian Press.

Ford, Jeffrey D. 1979. "Institutional versus Questionnaire Measures of Organizational Structure: A Reexamination." *Academy of Management Journal* 22 (September):601–610.

Frarey, C. J. 1953. "Studies of Use of the Subject Catalog: Summary and Evaluation." In *Subject Analysis of Library Materials*, ed. M. F. Tauber. New York: School of Library Service, Columbia University.

Friedlander, F., and H. Pickle. 1968. "Components of Effectiveness in Small Organizations." *Administrative Science Quarterly* 13:289–304.

Georgopolous, Basil S., and Arnold S. Tannenbaum. 1957. "The Study of Organizational Effectiveness." *American Sociological Review* 22:534–540.

Gibeon, J. L., J. M. Ivancevich, and J. H. Donnelly. 1973. *Organizations: Structure, Processes, Behavior*. Dallas, Tex.: Business Publications.

Goldhor, H. 1973. "Analysis of an Inductive Method of Evaluating the Book Collection of a Public Library." *Libri* 23:6–17.

———. 1981. "A Report on an Application of the Inductive Method of Evaluation of Public Library Books." *Libri* 31:121–129.

Goodman, P. S. 1979. "Organizational Effectiveness as a Decision Making Process." Paper presented at the 39th Annual Meeting of the Academy of Management, Atlanta, Ga.

Goodman, P. S., and J. M. Pennings, eds. 1980. "Critical Issues in Assessing Organizational Effectiveness." In *Organizational Assessment Perspectives on the Measurement of Organizational Behavior and the Quality of Work Life*, ed. E. E. Lawler, D. A. Nadler, and C. Cammann. New York: Wiley.

Goodman, Paul S., and Johannes M. Pennings, eds. 1977. *New Perspectives on Organizational Effectiveness*. San Francisco: Jossey-Bass.

Goodman, Paul S., Robert S. Atkin, and F. David Schoorman. 1983. "On the Demise of Organizational Effectiveness Studies." In *Organizational Effectiveness: A Comparison of Multiple Models*, ed. Kim S. Cameron and David A. Whetten, 163–183. Orlando, Fla.: Academic Press.

Gorman, M. 1968. *A Study of the Rules for Entry and Heading in the Anglo-American Cataloging Rules, 1967*. London: Library Association.

Greenberg, Douglas. 1991. "Information Access: Our Elitist System Must Be Reformed." *Chronicle of Higher Education* 38 (October 23):A48.

Gross, E. 1968. "Universities as Organizations: A Research Approach." *American Sociological Review* 33:518–544.

Gupta, Anil. 1965. "Contingency Linkages Between Strategy and General Manager Characteristics: A Conceptual Examination." *Academy of Management Review* 9:399–412.

Haberstroh, Chadwick J. 1965. "Organizational Design and Systems Analysis." In *Handbook of Organizations*, ed. James G. March. Chicago: Rand McNally.

Hackman, J. R. 1977. "Work Design." In *Improving Life at Work: Behavioral Science Approaches to Organizational Change*, ed. J. R. Hackman and J. L. Suttle. Santa Monica, Calif.: Goodyear.

Hall, Richard H. 1972. *Organizations: Structure and Process*. Englewood Cliffs, N.J.: Prentice-Hall.

———. 1978. "Conceptual, Methodological, and Moral Issues in the Study of Organizational Effectiveness." Working paper, Department of Sociology, State University of New York at Albany.

Hamburg, M., et al. 1974. *Library Planning and Decision-Making Systems*. Cambridge, Mass.: MIT Press.

Hamburg, M., E. Ramist, and M.R.W. Bommer. 1972. "Library Objectives and Performance Measures and Their Use in Decision Making." *Library Quarterly* 42:107–128.

Hardesty, L. 1981. "Use of Library Materials at a Small Liberal Arts College." *Library Research* 3:261–282.

Hartigan, John A. 1975. *Clustering Algorithms*. New York: Wiley.

Hernon, Peter. 1987. "Utility Measures, Not Performance Measures, for Library Reference Service?" *RQ* 26:449–459.

Hershfield, Allen F. 1972. "Measuring Library Effectiveness: A Challenge to Library Education." In *Approaches to Measuring Library Effectiveness: A Symposium*. *See* Hershfield and Boone, 1972.

Hershfield, Allen F., and Morrell D. Boone, eds. 1972. *Approaches to Measuring Library Effectiveness: A Symposium*. Syracuse, N.Y.: Syracuse University School of Library Science.

Hirsch, Paul M. 1975. "Organizational Effectiveness and the Institutional Environment." *Administrative Science Quarterly* 20:327–344.

Hopkins, Francis L. 1981. "User Instruction in the College Library: Origins, Prospects, and a Practical Program." In *College Librarianship*, ed. William Miller and D. Stephen Rockwood. Metuchen, N.J.: Scarecrow Press.

Hoy, Frank, David D. Van Fleet, and Marvin J. Yetley. 1984. "Comparative Organizational Effectiveness Research Leading to an Intervention Strategy." *Journal of Management Studies* 21 (December):443–462.

Hrebiniak, Lawrence G. 1978. *Complex Organizations*. St. Paul, Minn.: West Publishing.

John Minter Associates. 1991. *Rankings: Selected Management Ratios. A Handbook for Classifying and Comparing Institutions*. Boulder, Colo.: John Minter Associates.

Johnson, B. Lamar. 1939. *Vitalizing a College Library*. Chicago: American Library Association.

Jones, K. H. 1976. "Creative Library Management." In *A Reader in Library Management*, ed. R. Shimmon. Hamden, Conn.: Linnet Books.

Kania, Antoinette M. 1988. "Academic Library Standards and Performance Measures." *College and Research Libraries* 49:16–23.

Kaplan, Abraham. 1964. *The Conduct of Inquiry*. Scranton, Pa.: Chandler.

Katz, Daniel, and David L. Kahn. 1978. *The Social Psychology of Organizations*. New York: Wiley.

Kaufman, Herbert. 1960. *The Forest Ranger*. Baltimore: Johns Hopkins University Press.

Keeley, M. 1978. "A Social Justice Approach to Organizational Evaluation." *Administrative Science Quarterly* 22:272–292.

Kent, Allen, and Thomas J. Galvin. 1977. *Library Resource Sharing*. New York: Marcel Dekker.

Kent, Allen, Jacob Cohen, K. Leon Montgomery, James G. Williams, Stephen Bulick, Roger Flynn, William Sabor, and Una Mansfield. 1979. *Use of Library Materials: The University of Pittsburgh Study*. New York: Dekker.

Kerlinger, F. N. 1973. *Foundations of Behavioral Research*. New York: Holt, Rhinehart, and Winston.

Khandwalla, Pradip N. 1977. *The Design of Organizations*. New York: Harcourt Brace Jovanovich.

Kim, Jae-On, and Charles W. Mueller. 1978. *Factor Analysis: Statistical Methods and Practical Issues*. Beverly Hills: Sage Publications.

Kimberly, J. R. 1976a. "Contingencies in the Creation of Organizations: An Example from Medical Education." Paper presented at the EIASM/Dansk Management Center Seminar on Entrepreneurs and the Process of Institution Building, Copenhagen, Denmark.

———. 1976b. "Organizational Size and the Structuralist Perspective: A Review, Critique, and Proposal." *Administrative Science Quarterly* 21:571–597.

Kimberly, J. R., M. J. Mistretta, and D. B. Rottman. 1975. "Environment, Organization and Effectiveness." Paper presented at the 70th Annual Meeting of the American Sociological Association, San Francisco.

Kirchoff, Bruce A. 1975. "Examination of a Factor Analysis as a Technique for Determining Organizational Effectiveness." Proceedings of Midwest AIDS Conference.

———. 1977. "Organizational Effectiveness Measurement and Policy Research." *Academy of Management Review* 1:347–355.

Knapp, Patricia B. 1966. *The Monteith College Library Experiment*. Metuchen, N.J.: Scarecrow Press.

Knightly, John J. 1979. "Overcoming the Criterion Problem in the Evaluation of Library Performance." *Special Libraries* 70:173–178.

Kraft, Donald H., and Bert R. Boyce. 1991. *Operations Research for Libraries and Information Agencies: Techniques for the Evaluation of Management Decisions Alternatives*. San Diego: Academic Press.

Kruskal, William H., and Judith M. Tanur, eds. 1978. *International Encyclopedia of Statistics*, vol. 1. New York: Free Press.

Lancaster, F. W. 1977. *The Measurement and Evaluation of Library Services*. Arlington, Va.: Information Resources Press.

———. 1988. *If You Want to Evaluate Your Library*. . . . Champaign: University of Illinois, Graduate School of Library and Information Sciences.

Lawler, Edward E., Douglas T. Hall, and Greg L. Oldham. 1974. "Organizational Climate: Relationship to Organizational Structure, Process, and Performance." *Organizational Behavior and Human Performance* 11:139–155.

Lawrence, Paul R., and Guy W. Lorsch. 1969. *Organization and Environment*. Homewood, Ill.: Irwin.

Leimkuhler, F. F. 1967. "The Bradford Distribution." *Journal of Documentation* 23:197–207.

———. 1969. "On Information Storage Models." In *Planning Library Services: Proceedings of a Research Seminar Held at the University of Lancaster, 9–11 July*

1969, ed. A. G. Mackenzie and I. M. Stuart. Lancaster, England: University of Lancaster Library.

———. 1979. "Operations Research: Applications to Library Management." In *Library Research Round Table: 1977 Research Forum Proceedings*, ed. Charles C. Curran. Ann Arbor, Mich.: University Microfilms.

Leimkuhler, F. F., and M. D. Cooper. 1971. "Analytical Models for Library Planning." *Journal of the American Society for Information Science* 22:390–398.

Leimkuhler, F. F., and J. G. Cox. 1964. "Compact Book Storage in Libraries." *Operations Research* 12:419–427.

Lewis, David W. 1986. "An Organizational Paradigm for Effective Academic Libraries." *College and Research Libraries* 47:337–353.

Library Effectiveness: A State of the Art. 1980. Papers from a 1980 American Library Association Preconference. Chicago: American Library Association.

Likert, Rensis. 1967. *The Human Organization*. New York: McGraw-Hill.

Lindblom, Charles E. 1959. "The Science of 'Muddling Through.' " *Public Administration Review* 19:79–88.

Lipetz, Ben-Ami. 1970. *User Requirements in Identifying Desired Works in a Large Library*. New Haven, Conn.: Yale University Library.

———. 1972. "Catalog Use in a Large Research Library." *Library Quarterly* 42:129–139.

Lorr, Maurice. 1983. *Cluster Analysis for Social Scientists*. San Francisco: Jossey-Bass.

Lupton, A. H. 1976. "States and Productivity in Higher Education: An Ill-defined Relationship." *Public Productivity Review* 2:56–62.

Lynch, Mary Jo, and Helen M. Eckard, eds. 1981. *Library Data Collection Handbook*. Chicago: American Library Association.

McDonald, Joseph A. 1987. "Academic Library Effectiveness: An Organizational Perspective." Ph.D. diss., Drexel University.

McDonald, Joseph A., and Lynda B. Micikas. 1990. "Collection Evaluation and Development by Syllabus Analysis: The Must-Ought-Could (MOC) Method." In *Acquisitions 90: Conference on Acquisitions, Budgets, and Collections Proceedings*, ed. David C. Genaway. Canfield, Ohio: Genaway and Associates.

———. 1992. "This Stuff's Not Contagious." *Proceedings*, ASCUE (Association of Small Computer Users in Education) 25th Annual Conference. Myrtle Beach, S.C.: ASCUE.

McInnis, R. M. 1972. "The Formula Approach to Library Size: An Empirical Study of Its Efficiency in Evaluating Research Collections." *College and Research Libraries* 33:190–198.

Macy, S. A., and P. H. Mirvis. 1976. "A Methodology for Assessment of Quality of Work Life and Organizational Effectiveness in Behavior-economic Terms." *Administrative Science Quarterly* 21:212–226.

Mahoney, T. A. 1967. "Managerial Perceptions of Organizational Effectiveness." *Management Science* 14:76–91.

Mahoney, T. A., and P. J. Frost. 1974. "The Role of Technology in Models of Organizational Effectiveness." *Organizational Behavior and Human Performance* 11:122–138.

Mahoney, T. A., and E. F. Weitzel. 1969. "Managerial Models of Organizational Effectiveness." *Administrative Science Quarterly* 14:357–365.

March, R. M., and H. Mannari. 1976. "Employee Performance in Japanese Firms: An Explanation." *Organization and Administrative Sciences* 7:89–105.

Marchant, M. P. 1971. "Participative Management As Related to Personnel Development." *Library Trends* 20:48–59.

———. 1976. *Participative Management in Academic Libraries*. Westport, Conn.: Greenwood Press.

Martell, C. 1972. "Administration: Which Way—Traditional Practice or Modern Theory?" *College and Research Libraries* 33:104–112.

Martin, D. D., W. F. Lewis, and T. T. Serey. 1985. "Personnel Managers' Perceptions of the Determinants of Organizational Effectiveness." *Akron Business and Economic Review* 16:19–23.

Maruyama, M. 1963. "The Second Cybernetics: Deviation-amplifying Mutual Causal Processes." *American Scientist* 51:164–179.

Mellon, Constance A., ed. 1987. *Bibliographic Instruction: The Second Generation*. Littleton, Colo.: Libraries Unlimited.

Merton, Robert K. 1957. *Social Theory and Social Structure*. New York: Free Press.

Middle States Association of Colleges and Schools, Commission on Higher Education. 1988. *Characteristics of Excellence in Higher Education: Standards for Accreditation*. Philadelphia: The Association.

Miksa, Francis. 1989. "The Future of Reference II: A Paradigm of Academic Library Organization." *College and Research Library News* 50 (October):780–790.

Miles, M. B. 1965. "Planned Change and Organizational Health, Figure and Ground." In *Change Processes in the Public Schools*, ed. Richard O. Carlson. Eugene, Oreg.: Center for the Advanced Study of Educational Administration, Oregon University.

Miles, R. H. 1980. *Macro-Organizational Behavior*. Santa Monica, Calif.: Goodyear.

Miles, R. H., and K. Cameron. 1982. *Coffin Nails and Corporate Strategies*. Englewood Cliffs, N.J.: Prentice-Hall.

Miles, R. H., and W. A. Randolph. 1980. "Influence of Organizational Learning Styles on Early Development." In *The Organizational Life Cycle*, ed. J. R. Kimberly and R. H. Miles. San Francisco: Jossey-Bass.

Miller, William, and D. Stephen Rockwood. 1981. "Collection Development from a College Perspective." In *College Librarianship*, ed. William Miller and D. Stephen Rockwood. Metuchen, N.J.: Scarecrow Press.

Mintzberg, Henry. 1979. *The Structuring of Organizations: A Synthesis of the Research*. Englewood Cliffs, N.J.: Prentice-Hall.

Molnar, J. J., and D. C. Rogers. 1976. "Organizational Effectiveness: An Empirical Comparison of the Goal and System Resource Approach." *Sociological Quarterly* 17:401–413.

Moran, Barbara B. 1984. *Academic Libraries: The Changing Knowledge Centers of Colleges and Universities*. ASHE-ERIC Higher Education Research Report No. 8. Washington, D.C.: Association for the Study of Higher Education.

Morse, P. 1968. *Library Effectiveness: A Systems Approach*. Cambridge, Mass.: MIT Press.

Mott, P. E. 1972. *The Characteristics of Effective Organizations*. New York: Harper and Row.

Murphy, Marcy. 1987. "Setting Goals for Organizational and Individual Achievement: An Overview." *Journal of Library Administration* 8:65–79.

Negandhi, A. R., and B. C. Reimann. 1973. "Task Environment, Decentralization and Organizational Effectiveness." *Human Relations* 26:203–214.

Norusis, Marija J. 1986. *SPSS PC+ Advanced Statistics*. Chicago: Statistical Package in the Social Sciences.

Nunnally, J. C. 1967. *Psychometric Theory*. New York: McGraw-Hill.

———. 1978. *Psychometric Theory*. New York: McGraw-Hill.

O'Neill, Edward T. 1984. "Operations Research." *Library Trends* 32:509–520.

Orr, Richard H. 1973. "Measuring the Goodness of Library Services: A General Framework for Considering Quantitative Measures." *Journal of Documentation* 29:315–332.

Orr, R. H., V. M. Pings, I. H. Pizer, and E. E. Olsen. 1968a. "Development of Methodologic Tools for Planning and Managing Library Services: I. Project Goals and Approach; II. Measuring a Library's Capability for Providing Documents." *Bulletin of the Medical Library Association* 56:235–267.

———. 1968b. "Development of Methodologic Tools for Planning and Managing Library Services: III. Standardized Inventories of Library Services." *Bulletin of the Medical Library Association* 56:380–403.

Orr, R. H., and A. P. Schless. 1972. "Document Delivery Capabilities of Major Biomedical Libraries in 1968: Results of a National Survey Employing Standardized Tests." *Bulletin of the Medical Library Association* 60:382–422.

Osburn, Charles B. 1979. *Academic Research and Library Resources*. Westport, Conn.: Greenwood Press.

Payne, R., and D. S. Pugh. 1976. "Organizational Structure and Climate." In *Handbook of Industrial and Organizational Psychology*, ed. M. D. Dunnette. Chicago: Rand McNally.

Pennings, J. M. 1973. "Measures of Organizational Structure: A Methodological Note." *American Journal of Sociology* 79:686–704.

———. 1975. "Dimensions of Organizational Influence and Their Effectiveness Correlations." *Administrative Science Quarterly* 20:393–410.

Pennings, Johannes M., and Paul S. Goodman. 1977. "Toward a Workable Framework," In *New Perspectives on Organizational Effectiveness*. *See* Goodman and Pennings, 1977.

Perrow, C. 1970. "Goals in Complex Organizations." *American Sociological Review* 6:845–865.

Pfeffer, Jeffrey. 1977. "Usefulness of the Concept." In *New Perspectives on Organizational Effectiveness*. *See* Goodman and Pennings, 1977.

Pfiffner, J. M., and F. P. Sherwood. 1960. *Administrative Organization*. Englewood Cliffs, N.J.: Prentice-Hall.

Pings, V. M. 1968. "Development of Quantitative Assessment of Medical Libraries." *College and Research Libraries* 29:373–380.

Postman, Neil. 1991. "Six Things Worth Knowing about Technology." *Cause/Effect* 14 (Fall):46–48.

Powell, Ronald R. 1988. *The Relationship of Library User Studies to Performance Measures: A Review of the Literature*. Champaign-Urbana: University of Illinois Graduate School of Library and Information Science.

Price, James L. 1968. *Organizational Effectiveness: An Inventory of Propositions*. Homewood, Ill.: Richard D. Irwin.

———. 1972. "The Study of Organizational Effectiveness." *Sociological Quarterly* 13:3–15.

Price, James L., and Charles W. Mueller. 1986. *Handbook of Organizational Measurement*. Marshfield, Mass.: Pitman Publishing.

Pritchard, A., M. Auckland, and M. E. Castens. 1971. *Library Effectiveness Study*. London: City of London Polytechnic, Library and Learning Resources Service.

Pritchard, A., and M. Auckland. 1972. *Library Effectiveness*. London: City of London Polytechnic.

Provan, Keith G., and David W. Stewart. 1984. "Relation Between Resource Acquisition and Effective Resource Use." *Evaluation Review* 18 (August):493–518.

Query, Lance. 1985. "Librarians and Teaching Faculty: Disparity within the System." *Academe* 71:16.

Quinn, Robert E., and Kim Cameron. 1983. "Organizational Life Cycles and Shifting Criteria of Effectiveness: Some Preliminary Evidence." *Management Science* 29:33–51.

Raffel, J. A., and R. Shishko. 1969. *Systematic Analysis of University Libraries: An Application of Cost Benefit Analysis to the M.I.T. Libraries*. Cambridge, Mass.: MIT Press.

Reimann, B. C. 1974. "Dimensions of Structure in Effective Organizations: Some Empirical Evidence." *Academy of Management Journal* 17:693–708.

Reinhart, U. E. 1973. "Proposed Changes in the Organization of Health Care Delivery: An Overview and Critique." *Milbank Memorial Fund Quarterly* 51:169–222.

Rice, A. K. 1963. *The Enterprise and Its Environment*. London, England: Tavistock.

Rice, C. E. 1961. "A Model for the Empirical Study of a Large Social Organization." *General Systems Yearbook* 6:101–106.

Robbins, Jane. 1991. "Cultural Authority Achieved through Specialization." *Journal of Academic Librarianship* 17:214–215.

Rogers, R. B. 1954. "Measurement and Evaluation." *Library Journal* 3:177–187.

Rowley, J. E., and P. J. Rowley. 1981. *Operations Research: A Tool for Library Management*. Chicago: American Library Association.

Rzasa, P. V., and N. R. Baker. 1972. "Measures of Effectiveness for a University Library." *Journal of the American Society for Information Science* 23 (July-August):248–253.

Salverson, C. A. 1969. "The Relevance of Statistics to Library Evaluation." *College and Research Libraries* 30:352–362.

Sathe, V. 1978. "Institutional Versus Questionnaire Measures of Organizational Structure." *Academy of Management Journal* 21:227–238.

Schmersahl, Carmen B. 1987. "Teaching Library Research: Process, Not Product." *Journal of Teaching and Writing* 6:231–238.

Schmidt, F. L., J. E. Hunter, and V. W. Urry. 1976. "Statistical Power in Criterion-Related Validation Studies." *Journal of Applied Psychology* 61:473–485.

Schneider, Benjamin, and Neal Schmitt. 1986. *Staffing Organizations*. Glenview, Ill.: Scott, Foresman.

Schwab, Donald P. 1986. "Construct Validity in Organizational Behavior." In *Research and Organizational Behavior*, vol. 2, ed. Barry M. Staw and Larry L. Cummings, 3–43. Greenwich, Conn.: JAI Press.

Scriven, Michael. 1967. "The Methodology of Evaluation." In *Perspectives of Curric-*

ulum Evaluation, ed. Ralph W. Tyler, Robert M. Gagne, and Michael Scriven. Chicago: Rand McNally.

Scott, W. Richard. 1977. "Effectiveness of Organizational Effectiveness Studies." In *New Perspectives on Organizational Effectiveness. See* Goodman and Pennings, 1977.

Seashore, S. E., B. P. Indik, and B. S. Georgopolous. 1960. "Relationships among Criteria of Job Performance." *Journal of Applied Psychology* 44:195–202.

Seber, G.A.F. 1984. *Multivariate Observations*. New York: Wiley.

Selltiz, Claire, Marie Jahoda, Morton Deutsch, and Stuart W. Cook. 1959. *Research Methods in Social Relations*. New York: Holt, Rhinehart, and Winston.

Shaughnessy, Thomas W. 1988. "Organizational Culture in Libraries: Some Management Perspectives." *Journal of Library Administration* 9:5–10.

Shaw, C. B. 1931. *A List of Books for College Libraries*. Chicago: American Library Association.

Shiflett, Orvin Lee. 1981. *Origins of American Academic Librarianship*. Norwood, N.J.: Ablex.

Staw, Barry M., and L. L. Cummings, eds. 1984. *Research in Organizational Behavior: An Annual Series of Analytical Essays and Critical Reviews*, vol. 6. Greenwich, Conn.: JAI Press.

Steers, Richard M. 1975. "Problems in the Measurement of Organizational Effectiveness." *Administrative Science Quarterly* 20 (December):546–558.

———. 1977. *Organizational Effectiveness: A Behavioral View*. Santa Monica, Calif.: Goodyear.

Swanson, D. R. 1972. "Requirements Study for Future Catalogs." *Library Quarterly* 42:302–315.

Tagliacozzo, Renata, and Manfred Kochen. 1970. "Information-Seeking Behavior of Catalogue Users." *Information Storage and Retrieval* 6:363–381.

Tagliacozzo, Renata, Lawrence Rosenberg, and Manfred Kochen. 1970. "Access and Recognition: From Users' Data to Catalogue Entries." *Journal of Documentation* 26:230–249.

Tatterdell, B., and J. Bird. 1976. *The Effective Library: Report of the Hillingdon Project on Public Library Effectiveness*. London, England: Library Association.

Taylor, Robert S. 1972. "Measuring the Immeasurable: Or Can We Get There from Here?" In *Approaches to Measuring Library Effectiveness: A Symposium. See* Hershfield and Boone, 1972.

Thompson, J. D. 1967. *Organizations in Action*. New York: McGraw-Hill.

Thorndike, Robert M. 1978. *Correlational Procedures for Research*. New York: Gardner Press.

Thurstone, L. L. 1947. *Multiple Factor Analysis*. Chicago: University of Chicago Press.

Trueswell, R. W. 1969. "User Circulation Satisfaction vs. Size of Holdings at Three Academic Libraries." *College and Research Libraries* 30:204–213.

University of Chicago Graduate Library School. 1968. *Requirements Study for Future Catalogues*. Progress Report No. 2. Chicago: University of Chicago.

"Vanderbilt's Chancellor: A Tireless Advocate for Computer Technology." *Chronicle of Higher Education* 38 (September 4):A28.

Van de Ven, A. H. 1977. "A Process for Organizational Assessment." Working paper, The Wharton School, University of Pennsylvania.

Van de Ven, A. H., and D. L. Ferry. 1980. *Measuring and Assessing Organizations.* New York: Wiley.

Van House, Nancy A., Beth T. Weil, and Charles R. McClure. 1990. *Measuring Academic Library Performance: A Practical Approach.* Prepared for the Association of College and Research Libraries Ad Hoc Committee on Performance Measures. Chicago: American Library Association.

Virgo, Julie Carroll, and David Allen Yuro, eds. 1981. *Libraries and Accreditation in Institutions of Higher Education: Proceedings of a Conference Held in New York City June 26–27, 1980.* Chicago: Association of College and Research Libraries.

Warner, W. Keith. 1967. "Problems in Measuring the Goal Attainment of Voluntary Organizations." *Journal of Adult Education* 19:3–14.

Webb, Ronald J. 1974. "Organizational Effectiveness and the Voluntary Organization." *Academy of Management Journal* 17:663–677.

Weick, Karl E. 1969. *The Social Psychology of Organizations.* Reading, Mass.: Addison-Wesley.

———. 1976. "Educational Organizations as Loosely Coupled Systems." *Administrative Science Quarterly* 21 (March):1–19.

———. 1977. "Re-Punctuating the Problem." In *New Perspectives on Organizational Effectiveness. See* Goodman and Pennings, 1977.

Weigand, Wayne A. 1986. "Perspectives on Library Education in the Context of Recently Published Literature on the History of Professions." *Journal of Education for Library and Information Science* 26 (Spring):267–280.

Werrell, Emily, and Laurel Sullivan. 1987. "Faculty Status for Academic Librarians: A Review of the Literature." *College and Research Libraries* 48:95–103.

Wessel, C. J., B. A. Cohrssen, and K. L. Moore. 1967–1969. *Criteria for Evaluating the Effectiveness of Library Operations and Services*, vols. 1–3. Washington, D.C.: John I. Thompson.

White, G. T. 1977. "Quantitative Measures of Library Effectiveness." *Journal of Academic Librarianship* 3:128–136.

Yuchtman, Ephraim, and Stanley E. Seashore. 1967. "A System Resource Approach to Organizational Effectiveness." *American Sociological Review* 32:891–903.

Zammuto, R. F. 1982. *Assessing Organizational Effectiveness: Systems Change, Adaptation, and Strategy.* Albany, N.Y.: SUNY-Albany Press.

INDEX

About the Authors

JOSEPH A. McDONALD was formerly Vice-President for Information Services at Dordt College, Sioux Center, Iowa. An authority on information systems design and management, his work has been published in journals such as *Drexel Library Quarterly*, *Library Software Review*, and *The Reformed Journal*.

LYNDA BASNEY MICIKAS is an Independent Consultant in Learning and Information in Denver. She is also Director of The Human Genome Project: Information Access, Management, and Regulation for the Biological Sciences Curriculum Study at Colorado Springs, Colorado. She was formerly an Associate Professor and Chair of Natural Sciences and Mathematics at Holy Family College.